AWAY WITH WORDS

Young Writers' 16th Annual Poetry Competition

It is feeling and force of imagination that make us eloquent.

How can I not dream while writing? The blank page gives a right to dream.

Scotland

Edited by Allison Jones

 Young**Writers**

Foreword

This year, the Young Writers' *Away With Words* competition proudly presents a showcase of the best poetic talent selected from thousands of up-and-coming writers nationwide.

Young Writers was established in 1991 to promote the reading and writing of poetry within schools and to the young of today. Our books nurture and inspire confidence in the ability of young writers and provide a snapshot of poems written in schools and at home by budding poets of the future.

The thought, effort, imagination and hard work put into each poem impressed us all and the task of selecting poems was a difficult but nevertheless enjoyable experience.

We hope you are as pleased as we are with the final selection and that you and your family continue to be entertained with *Away With Words Scotland* for many years to come.

Contents

Leighann Combe (12)   45
Alexander MacLeod (13)   45
Lauren Henderson & Natalie Mackay (15)   46
Emily Fulton (12)   46
David Duncan (16)   47
Bronwen Winter (13)   48
Bethany Winter (15)   49
Sarah Finlay (13)   49
Zoe Sayers (13)   50
Kevin Reid (14)   50
Lauren Snedden (13)   51
Taylor McIntyre (13)   52
Hannah Rose (13)   53
Rebekah Smart (13)   54

Brae High School, Brae

Sam Laurenson (13)   54
Martha Morton (12)   55
Josie Leask (12)   55
Rowan Johnson (12)   55
Becky Rees (13)   56

Broughton High School, Edinburgh

Laura Hunter (14)   56
Zainab Hussain (14)   57
Fergus Cook (14)   57
Anja Campbell-McConnachie (14)   58
Gina Cameron (13)   58
Alice Bremner Watt (15)   59
Rebecca Black (14)   59
Alan Troake (14)   60
Ewan Zuckert (14)   60
Andrew Vernon (14)   61
Calum Macleod (15)   61
Rosie Shillinglaw (14)   62
Clarke Veitch (14)   62
Kelsie Stevenson (14)   63
Amanda Laurenson (14)   63
Jordan McKenzie (14)   64
Jodie Robertson (14)   64
Claire Ross (14)   65

Hannah Mawhinney (13)	87
Colin Harper (13)	88
Greg Laird (13)	89
Lindsay Campbell (13)	89
Nikola Zikic (13)	90
Elliot Whitnall (12)	91
Sarah Semple (13)	92
Fiona Gemmell (13)	93
Ainsley Miller (13)	94
Andrew Baldacci (12)	95
Natalie Duncanson (13)	96

Gordonstoun School, Elgin
Pippa Janssenswillen (16)	97

Greenock High School, Greenock
Gail Fulton (16)	98
William McGeachy (14)	99
Joseph Craig (14)	100
Elaine Willdridge (17)	101

Harris Academy, Dundee
Miriam Chappell (13)	102
Naushin Nawar (13)	103
Susannah Cummins (13)	104
Ewan Patterson (13)	104
Joanna Bone (13)	105
Ruqueia Ossman (13)	106
Hannah Kane (13)	107
Anna Grinev (13)	108
Tara Matthews (13)	109
Sarra El-Wahed (13)	110
Mhairi Fenton (13)	110
Tom Walkinshaw (13)	111
Sarah Menzies (13)	111
Isra Al-Saffar (14)	112
Hester Astell (13)	112
Fiona Leslie (13)	113
Emily Spasic (13)	114
Channelle Buchan (14)	115
Jane Caird (13)	115

The Poems

Greenland

The Northern Lights shine red and green
You won't believe what you have seen!
Just look up into the skies
You've got to see with your own eyes!

The Inuit are native people from Greenland
They have to live with ice, no sun or sand!
Inuits build igloos from lots of snow
There's no hot place, it's cold everywhere you go!

Polar bears can swim for ages without a break
They wait for dinner, how long will it take?
Polar bears' fur looks white but it's see-through
The cubs stay with their mother till they're two.

Greenland is the world's largest island
There's millions of things to do in this wintry wonderland.
I wouldn't like to meet a humpback whale
If you go in a kayak watch where you sail!

Lauren Greer (11)

Haikus

Mountains
Tower of dark stone
Their tops pierce the high heavens
Higher than all things.

The Sea
Waters cold and dark
Swallowing lands under waves
Drowning life and joy.

Andrew Gardyne (15)
Aboyne Academy, Aboyne

Sun - Gone

Torches make perfect circles on walls,
Albino-white faces like those of dolls,
The church clock chimes, six hours till one,
The huge industrial lights switch on.

Bells on walls start to ring-ring,
A mechanical bird begins to sing
Blocks of lines march across the concrete,
Only sound is that of stamping feet.

The clock ticks, twelve hours is done,
Another twelve hours of dark till the lights switch on
Torches make perfect circles on walls
Albino-white faces like those of dolls.

Holly Phimister (14)
Aboyne Academy, Aboyne

Foundations

Once the wax has melted,
The teenage skin lies bare,
The blemishes and imperfections,
Reveal it if you dare.

The lightly balding eyebrows
The wild orange mask
The streaming blackened eyelashes
Foundations built to last.

Burning tongs and tweezers
Provide torture for the head
Till each face is constricted
And all expression dead.

With her mane about her shoulders
And her skirt above her thighs,
She thinks she paints foundation,
But she's only painting lies.

Megan Albon (14)
Aboyne Academy, Aboyne

Misunderstood

She is but a breath of wind,
That dances out of control.
Knowing that her past has sinned,
They tear holes in her fragile soul.

She cowers back behind her mask,
Hiding behind a tainted smile.
False remarks and jeering laughs,
What you say's not what they hear.

Another day, a brand new trend,
Fix your smile, paint on a face,
When will the undeserving torture end?
Shrink away, escape this place.

Forcing wires into her ears,
Brainwashed by the tactful lyrics.
Head bowed low, gaze averted,
Shutting her identity out of view.

Hannah Goddard (14)
Aboyne Academy, Aboyne

Entre Acte

Pulse thumps,
Blood pumps,
The curtains unravel,
The scene's story begins to travel,
Eyelids flicker,
Lights shimmer,
Personality hidden,
Theatre arts manifest,
Misleading from reality,
The place of human sanity,
Insecurity demolished,
Characters well polished,
The real soul abolished.

Lindsay Atherton (14)
Aboyne Academy, Aboyne

Echoes

The wind whistles through the trees
As if letting out a long low sigh
Thin branches swayed in the breeze
As the leaves rustled their reply.

Sad mournful voices moan all around
Nothing stirred but the wind
Moonlight pale upon the ground
And all who came and saw were sinned.

The trees bathed in a milky glow
Murmurs from days gone past
Spirits and echoes from long ago
Looking for peace to rest at last.

Now quiet, dark, still
Cut the air with a knife
Ice, sharp, deathly chill
End of memories, end of life.

Laura-Jane Fyfe (14)
Aboyne Academy, Aboyne

Double Haiku

I saw a black sky
Above the alien Earth
And I was alone.

You entered my life
The universe erupted
A billion stars.

Lauren Anderson (14)
Aboyne Academy, Aboyne

The Hermit Crab

The hermit crab he scuttles along
His giant shell, pointy and round
His pincers sharp and ready to kill

The hermit crab he scuttles along
A bird swoops down and pecks at his shell
Peck, peck, peck! The shell won't break

The hermit crab he scuttles along
He walks into the sea
He walks very far through the sea and the sand

The hermit crab he scuttles along
He gets trapped in a net all holey and round
He moves and he moves but he cannot get out

The hermit crab he scuttles no more
He lies there dead in the fisherman's boat
His beautiful shell to be put on a shelf.

William Nicholass-McKee (15)
Aboyne Academy, Aboyne

Bike

She handles like a real dream
The sun makes her shine and gleam
I race her through the deepest streams
Until the engine starts to steam.
I race her over the highest jumps
She speeds over the hills and bumps
She scrambles through the dirt bike track
Then we come home filthy black
I love to race my bike around
Tearing up the muddy ground.

Christopher Dunbar (13)
Aboyne Academy, Aboyne

Your Dreams, My Eyes

Whenever you're asleep,
Whenever you're awake
You think about me all day
And I'm in the dreams you make.

You love me, yet you hate me,
You don't know what to do.
But when you see my face
You know that I should be with you.

You want me to come closer
And yet you feel so scared
You think that you are going crazy
And that your vision is impaired.

You need me and you want me,
But am I really real?
You are slightly apprehensive,
You really don't know how you feel.

Your eyes move to meet mine,
You're now as confident as can be
But now that I get nearer
You try to run away from me.

You're running and I'm chasing,
You don't know what to do.
So you turn around and hug me,
You want me to be with you.

You fall down to the ground,
I kiss you one last time.
I run away and leave you, knowing
Forever you'll be mine.

Joe Scotchman (14)
Aboyne Academy, Aboyne

Rabbit

6 o'clock, the sun is rising
I'm up and about,
Munching on green, green grass.

I hear a sound,
I stand up on my back feet,
With my ears up tall,
'Oh, it's a bird,' I say to myself.

People scare me,
So do cars
But I'll be OK if
I don't go on roads.

I'm like a hare,
My nose twitches day and night
I'm super at hearing
And I'm a fast runner too.

Jumping through the long grass
That's my favourite thing to do
I also like to eat.

I like my life,
I really do,
Eat all day,
Sleep all night.

People say I'm cute,
Of course I am,
I'm a rabbit.

Nikki Forbes (13)
Aboyne Academy, Aboyne

Blue Monday

The sky is grey
The pavement so
The gutter black
As hooded death
The windowpane
Is clear as snow
Melted on the breeze
Yet people wonder
All the time
Or so I'm told
In blatant tone
Why stay inside?
An average day
Is really not
That great in winter hours
And so I feel
It's quite all right
To be a little sour.

Jake Morris (14)
Aboyne Academy, Aboyne

No Ice, No Seals, No Home

Swimming, always swimming
No more ice for me to stroll over
I am swinging, swinging
Towards a tumbling death
No ice, no seals, no snow.

Too tired to swim so I float
My legs are like jelly
And there is nothing in my belly
I lie and I cry, why no ice? why, why?
I live my final moment floating in the cold
No ice, no seals, no home.

Ronan Collins (13)
Aboyne Academy, Aboyne

Dylan

D ylan is my nephew
Y es, he loves to run around
L ovely as he is, he loves to do mischief
A s he eats his tea he loves to giggle and chatter
N othing else makes me laugh like his little face

I f he runs out of things to do, he finds something else to do
S mall, but yet so tall

G reetings he gives are so much fun
R unning around the house with so much energy
E ating his dinner he sits at the table with pride
A t this time he is nearly two
T aking his time, he is the best.

Charlie Myron (13)
Aboyne Academy, Aboyne

I Wish I Were . . .

I wish I were a turtle
I'd live for many years
I could swim in the deep blue ocean
And walk the sandy shores.

I wish I were a shark
Feared by all the fish in the sea
I could do whatever I pleased
And no one would bother me!

I wish I were a cat
I'd prowl around the forest
I could catch a bird or a rat for my supper
And go to my house for a cosy nap.

I wish I were a monkey
Think of all the fun I'd have
I could swing from tree to tree
And gorge myself with fruit and berries.

Christina Menzies (14)
Aboyne Academy, Aboyne

The Deep Blue Sea

In the deep blue sea
Where the scuba-divers like to be
Discovering what there is to see
Like sharks and whales across the reef
Seaweed and mermaids dangled in pearls
All the pirates and treasure in the world
Oh, what it would be like
To live in the deep blue sea.

Iona Yule (13)
Aboyne Academy, Aboyne

The Lost Dog

I used to have a home
In the middle of a town
I used to be loved
Now I've been shoved
I'm lost in the world
I don't have food
Worst of all I'm cold and wet
Someone came and took me away to the RSPCA
Now I'm loved and cared for again.

Kristina Donald (13)
Aboyne Academy, Aboyne

Footprints

Dark and deep, the footprints lie
Sunk, printed into the ground
Only a trace to be found
Big and small they leave a trail
Across the sandy beach.

Paula Ferguson (13)
Aboyne Academy, Aboyne

Dolphins Of The Deep

Beautiful dolphins swimming in the sea
How many of them can you see?
1, 2, 3!

Blue, grey, black or white,
Jumping and jigging
With all their might.

A flash of a fin, a tail in the air
Then a splash and splosh
There's a dolphin out there!

So smooth and so silky,
They cut through the sea
Without any effort at all
They are as free as can be.

To watch them fly
Is a beautiful thing
Let's keep it that way
Let them swim free!

So many dolphins
Swimming in the sea
How many of them can you see?
1, 2, 3!

Gayle Main (12)
Armadale Academy, Armadale

Identity

My identity, me?
Well, I'll tell you
Oh come on
Hey, it's nae big secret
I willnae be angry
If you forget tae keep it.

I love music, drawing and books
To be awfully honest,
I don't concentrate on looks
All the other girls say
That I'm crazy and strange
And won't look good any day.

I like to sing and act,
I can be a bit strange.
Trust me, that's a fact
I can be funny and happy
Or quiet and sad
But it's not that bad.

I like black and purple
Dark colours are the best.
I have a really cool necklace,
That I wear on my chest.
I can be pretty gloomy at times
And I can make up sad rhymes.

I dream of everything,
Of the world, of me, of you.
Oh, and I'll tell you somethin'
Some of it's true!
But now I must go
Even though I've just said hello.

So I'll just say goodbye
Adios, see ya!
Oh and don't stop dreamin'
It's what makes ya you.
Well ta-ta, it's time to go,
Hey, don't you look at me and say 'so'.

'Cause yer identity's you
Ya know what I'm sayin'
Look, no one's the same
Not even me and you.
Besides, you rule yer own world,
Um, well apart from yer parents.

Nikki McDonald (12)
Armadale Academy, Armadale

Nature

The land is full of nature, as full as it can be
To know the world has creatures and birds that we can see,
Is a great comfort to us that we have the key,
To the nature of Earth helping you and me.

The trees and the plants and the flowers that grow,
That you care about us really nice to know,
Watering them and keeping them alive,
Our job is to make sure they survive.

In springtime we hear the birds tweeting loud
And the chicks popping out and making lots of sound.
The rabbits that sniff all around
And the people that realise spring has been found.

Emma Rintoul (12)
Armadale Academy, Armadale

My Identity

Charie Chazam -
That's what they all shout,
Except for my teachers
Who make them cut it out.

I'm only twelve
But I'm fairly tall
And, well, all of my friends
They're often quite small.

I've quite a lot of freckles
And I have curly hair,
Which most of the time
I can hardly bear.

I stay in Armadale
(That's where I'm from)
But Livingston is the place
Where I was born.

I try to look good
But don't overdo it
As I don't like it much
And then I just lose it.

My favourite hobby is dancing
I do hip hop, jazz and tap
And usually when I come home
I have to take a nap.

I like to go abroad -
I went there last year -
And love to meet friends
Who are usually not near.

I love going on my laptop,
I could stay on all night,
But usually I get told to come off
So I have to start a fight.

I like to play music,
I have my own bass,
And I carry it to school
In its big black case.

Well, there you go,
A bit about me
I'm sure if you meet me
You will clearly see.

So you can go away now
'Cause you will not see me
'Cause all that's left there
Is my identity.

Charmain Leitch (12)
Armadale Academy, Armadale

The Secret Of The Paintbrushes' Slimming Success

Five paintbrushes were waiting in a tub
Thinking about last night at the pub,
The number ten brush stood up and sighed,
'I'm far too fat,' he wailed and cried!
'If only I hadn't drunk so much beer
And I've gained a stone I fear!'

Then, up stood number eight,
Who couldn't fit through her garden gate,
She was determined to lose weight,
After her party, it would be too late.

In a small corner quivered bony number six,
She looked like she was made of sticks,
But she wanted a modelling life so bad,
She took a big risk, which was rather sad.

The next brush to confess was number four
(Who looked like she could eat a bit more).
In her opinion she was fat,
That stuck in her mind and that was that.

Two wanted to make herself heard,
She made the other brushes tune into every word,
'My modelling agency phoned yesterday,
Said I'd just make the cut, but you'd have to go away,
Unless of course, you shrink to size two,
For you five, that'd be hard to do.'

Later on, this skinny bunch
Thought about this over lunch,
'I know, we'll give her grief,' said four, munching on a lettuce leaf.
'Yes, but what do you mean?' said six pushing away her salad cream.

'Well bring two, plus twelves and up, all to the pub
Get them the nicest jacuzzi tub,
Fill it with bubbles, fill it with wine,
A bottle of Jacob's Peak will do just fine.'

While the group devised their devious plan
Brush two was in Florida getting her tan
They phoned two, to say they didn't want to fight,
They were sorry and would send her a party invite.

It was 8 o'clock on the night of the do
Thirty brushes appeared, waiting in the queue
Brush two was there, just as to plan
Envious eyes looked at her golden tan.
When the whistle blew, the brushes gave a shriek,
Men brushes guzzled beer,
Women gave a cheer,
Off popped the cork of Jacob's Peak.

The group heard number two
Singing loudly in the loo.
Of course, she'd had too much to drink
She'd forgotten about her modelling life and started to jive
The five slender brushes, saw their work was done
And landed each other with a big high five.

Months passed, the brushes gave up hope, but then . . .
Modelling contracts arrived for brushes four to ten.
Seems they were the only slim brushes in the land,
Paintbrush two, now so overweight, had been banned.

This story shows that it's not cool to get drunk every night,
You'll gain lots of weight and get involved in a fight.
The secret of the paintbrushes' slimming success will now be revealed,
I will tell you, but keep your lips sealed.

Why, the skinny brushes used the booze as bait
And tricked the other brushes into gaining weight.

Amy Green (13)
Balerno High School, Balerno

I Write

I write
I write to breathe
I write to breathe in this
I write to breathe in this foreboding cell
I write to breathe in this foreboding cell where the death
I write to breathe in this foreboding cell where the death of thousands
I write to breathe in this foreboding cell where the death of thousands
is glossed over
I write to breathe in this foreboding cell where the death of thousands
is glossed over like a trivial matter
I write to breathe in this foreboding cell where the death of thousands
is glossed over like a trivial matter just so
I write to breathe in this foreboding cell where the death of thousands
is glossed over like a trivial matter just so you can have one more
I write to breathe in this foreboding cell where the death of thousands
is glossed over like a trivial matter just so you can have one more
paid holiday
I write to breathe in this foreboding cell where the death of thousands
is glossed over like a trivial matter just so you can have one more
paid holiday in *your* paradise.

Roisin Kelly (12)
Balfron High School, Balfron

'Til The Morning

Through the glazed eyes, is a working mind.
Through the tangle of wires and machines, an active body.
A cheery face, once so happy,
Has now a still motionless stare.

Seeing you lie there, tears spring to my eyes.
The thought of you gone is too hard to accept.
As the weeks trudged by, seeing no change,
A hopeful thought lingered, but began to fade.

And now you're gone, no more pain, suffering or waiting.
You're at peace, just resting, sleeping.
Waiting for the day to live again.
That is the hope that keeps me strong.

Though I'm sad and angry, I know I'll see you again
In your full strength, glory and your face creased with smiles.
With your eyes sparkling in the bright new morning sun
There will be tears, not of sadness, but of joy and laughter.

Yvonne Bauwens (17)
Balfron High School, Balfron

Christabel Pankhurst: Dreaming

Dreaming again
In my cold jail cell
Dreaming about food
About air
About being alive
I can hear Mother protesting
In the next cell down
Squawking officiously about Women's Lib
And inequality
Queen of the Mob, they've named me
And yet she still scares me
Shouting
Screaming
Smacking furiously
Women's Lib for everyone but me
I am not yet free
From the pressure of her
I am protester, editor, writer and nurse
To her every whim and need
I refuse, I rebel, I disown
But I'll never tell her so . . .

Christine Stark (13)
Balfron High School, Balfron

To A Mouse/Louse

Aww! My lovely son,
A poet! Who'd have thought it!
If you'd told me when he was young,
I'd never have bought it.

Now he's rich and famous,
To think that I'm his mother!
You know that I am just so pleased,
He didn't turn out a thug like his brother.

Gah! My fool of a son,
A poet! A dandy!
If you ask me it was all his mum
How could my son be a pansy?

Even when he was ploughing the fields,
'Twas words that filled his head
The hardest work he does in a day
Is climb out of his four-poster bed.

Still, his money could look after us,
When we're too old to work the farm,
And think of the grandchildren staying with us
I guess it's not too much harm.

Fergus Evans (14)
Balfron High School, Balfron

Perseus

They strike down streets, the sisters three
With looks that turn to stone
All who argue pay the price
A life upon a plinth
Features defined by pigeon mess
And piles of long-dead leaves.

I avoided them at first
Lurking in shadows when they came
Slipping into alleys, dodging their stare
Till one day King Polydectes held
A feast, a banquet of such grace
To charm the lovely Hippodamia
A horse 'twas the payment to
All who came.

But I, great Perseus, wanted
To give something better
A loathsome sister's head
Medusa - the only mortal one
Who walked along
She was the worst
Features strewn haphazardly on her face
Cruel lips, twisted into a permanent look of hatred
Tomorrow the snakes around her head
Will cease to hiss.

Amy Graydon (13)
Balfron High School, Balfron

Paris' Mission

So many men are fighting
So many swords and knives
So many broken shields
So many shattered lives.

But it is me I take the shot,
The battle rages still
A hundred thousand battling me
And only one to kill.

My target is Achilles
My mission to destroy
This my most important act
At the terrible battle of Troy.

I pull my bow back gently
I search the violent crowd
The battlefield darkens
Underneath a huge black cloud.

The sound of rain on armour
Fills the cold clean air
I hear a voice which yells his name
Achilles must be near.

I see him, running closer
His eyes as cold as steel
I raise my bow, I take the shot
And hit Achilles' heel.

Josh Bird (14)
Balfron High School, Balfron

The Rock And Roll King

The rock and roll king that loved to perform,
The king that loved to sing,
A king that could also act as well,
The king that starred in successful films,
A king that cared about his wife and daughter,
The king that influenced thousands,
A king with record-selling tours,
The king that came from a small city,
A king that loved pop and country music,
Some kings can rule,
Other kings demand,
But this one can rock and roll,
Elvis is the king that can rock and roll.

Beth Grant (13)
Balfron High School, Balfron

Scar

He was always the dark one,
Quiet, wild and scarred
To be his little sister
I was very scared.

He roared like our older brother,
Though no one seemed to bother
Because he was not the king
I'm glad.

He was jealous and angry
Which made me want to hide
And when he threw a tantrum
My fear came like the tide.

Now he is dead
And took away my dread
He cannot roar
Because Scar is here no more.

Aimi Li (14)
Balfron High School, Balfron

I Watch

I watch as friendships erode
And others grow strong.

I watch as groups divide
And others form.

I watch as storm clouds brew
And skies begin to clear.

I watch as anger explodes
And apologies are exchanged.

I watch as friends leave
And never return.

I watch as tolerant faces laugh
At jokes they do not find funny.

I watch as intolerant faces twist
And contort in anger.

I watch as my whole world changes,
And I drag my heels against it.

Gareth Davey (16)
Balfron High School, Balfron

Mother Nature

Crashing white waves of destruction
Rise up like a roaring lion
About to leave millions of families
In desperate despair.
Towering waves come crashing
Around defenceless souls.
Despairing spirits lost,
Drowned, lie in thirsty graves.
An horrific natural weapon of mass destruction,
Torturing happiness and leaving dreadful suffering.
Holidays bringing pain instead of pleasure
by Mother Nature's cruel hand.

Rae Wilson (14)
Banff Academy, Banff

Day Of Dejection

The sky, murderous and depressed,
looms threateningly
over the deep, murky sea.
Shrapnel plunges heavily
on its dark, icy surface.
Soldiers are sitting despondently,
waiting in vain expectation
for their platoon to come.
Their hair is unbrushed and heavy,
their stomachs churning
but all they can do it wait
with forlorn hope
for their saviour.
Too weary to trench onwards,
because of aching feet.
Food is withering lower
like their every ounce of hope.
Water is quickly disappearing,
like their faith in being found.
All of their optimism
is turning into pessimism
full of hatred and disgust
towards the Nazis.
They wait stoically
as a plane glides past silently,
bearing the Nazi cross
as nullifying explosions are heard.

Ben Cole (14)
Banff Academy, Banff

Passport To Death

The pistol points deadly in its potential
Triggers to death's grave
A tunnel into the unknown path
The gleaming gun held
By a hand of wealth
Fingers heavy with gold
A fortune from fraud, fights and fatalism!
The stance of power
But this killer has no face
Covered with a hooded veil of darkness
This killer has no emotion
Blind to consequences
Fearless of their own
An occupation that has no mercy!
Streetlights spotlight
Highlighting this gangster
Yet he remains faceless!
In the background there is nothing
Nothing to see, hear or even touch.
A tasteless plot
Contained in an empty atmosphere,
With only this murderer
About to take from his victim
The passport of life!

Siobhan Mutch (14)
Banff Academy, Banff

Shared Concentration

A young couple stand
In shared concentration.
As they hug gently,
Their thoughts inevitably
On the unbearable separation to come.
Her smooth cheek rests on his soft shoulder.
The smell of her perfume
Makes him reluctant to let go.
A single tear falls slowly
From her closed eye.
Her mouth tugs down at the corners,
Signs of the current heartache
And the grief yet to come.
A ring on her finger
Glints like a watching eye.
Her hand clutches his jacket,
Green, brown, black.
His hand holds a strap
Which contains a cold, hard,
Metal weapon,
Bullets loaded, ready to fire.
A row of reinforced jeeps
Await the troops behind the couple,
Ready to set off to battle
When will they meet again?

Ashley Duguid (14)
Banff Academy, Banff

Scissors Through Paper

Fangs bared, deadly and ready,
Poised and streamlined.
Like a bear-trap,
Ready to close on its victim.
Saliva of anticipation drooling from its mouth
Lunging forward.
The atmospheric tradition of the hunt
Wavering throughout.
The other
Soon to meet the inevitable
Making one last desperate bid for life.
Bringing back its legs to gain momentum.
Snap, the trap sets off.
The scrambling of paws
The smell of desperation
The merciless dog's fangs
Sinking into skin,
As easy as scissors through paper
Movement dies as the proud hunter
Takes the blood-drenched corpse to its master.

Rachel Annand (14)
Banff Academy, Banff

Numb

A solitary fireman stands,
Dazed and confused,
His thoughts still,
Trapped in the atmosphere of grief and pain.
The young man can no longer keep up a front
His ears ring from violent screams of lost innocence,
But it's the living victims whose whimpers destroy him.
His eyes are black, not from injuries,
But from unthinkable disappointment and despair.
Now an exhausted and limp shadow,
He stands surrounded,
By a toxic mushroom of bitter smoke.
No longer does a powerful
Colossal building tower behind him
Only dust, rubble
And twisted jagged metal strips remain.
As the numb fireman,
Stands in the remains.

Kelsey Christie (14)
Banff Academy, Banff

Javelin

Shooting pains soar up her leg,
As the staying javelin skewers her foot,
Piercing her flesh,
Until the pain ascends throughout her body.
Unable to touch her foot,
She tightly grasps her leg,
Until she can stand it no more,
Her grimace revels distress and anguish,
As the javelin punctures her,
Like a nail in a car wheel,
Draining all the energy from her.
People rush to aid her,
Comforting and calming her,
But she is oblivious to this,
Huddled on the damp grass.
Gasps from the shocked crowd echo
Their disbelief and amazement,
At this bizarre event.

Kathryn Hay (14)
Banff Academy, Banff

The Bullring

The bull's sharp horn tears
Through the man's innocent leg.
A loud crack rings out
As the horn collides with hard bone.
Blood erupts from the man's deep wound
As the bull shakes him off his horn like a fly.
The beast stands primed
Awaiting the man's next move.
His face now contorts with pain
As he screams in horror.
The crowd scream in delight
At the bloodshed.
In the background, two paramedics
Rush to help the now unconscious man
As the bull lies tranquillised
In a deep dream of delight.

Iain McKean (14)
Banff Academy, Banff

Eternity

The Titanic cliffs continue into the endless distance
Blanketed white fog like soft snow
The rock giants collapse into the bottomless azure
While pillowy snow suffocates the hillsides
Birds chirp in the distance
The colossal timeless abyss
Reaches to the far-flung horizon
The old man on the outcrop
Is gazing at the wild scenery
As the chilled spring air gently brushes
His thick white jumper
Swathed and hugged around him
The perfect peace and warmth
Is breezing through his mind
As he is alone
In eternity.

Andrew Davidson (15)
Banff Academy, Banff

Towering Skyscrapers

Angry flames erupt and roar
Scorching surrounding surfaces.
A blinding orange fire
Floods the atmosphere.
Once towering skyscrapers
Now smash downwards,
As bulky boulders bounce off the ground.
Below pedestrians stare upwards
In amazement, shock, then fear,
Their innocent flesh slashed by glass
Then bruised by rubble.
They stumble about in heartbreaking pain.
Petrified shrieks and pained screams deafen the scene.
Thick choking smoke belches
In ever thickening eddies
Above the crashing twin buildings.

Zoe Findlay (14)
Banff Academy, Banff

Flight

An enormous stallion
Frantically gallops through the
Treacherous deep flood
Kicking and scrambling
With every movement.
His strong body hits
The water with extreme
Impact sending out splashes
And ripples.
Hundreds of horses surround him,
Some of them falling and
Drowning.
The smell of dirty water
Mixed with the sweaty smell
Of horses makes them panic
As they frantically belt.
Led by two saviours on huge steeds,
Trying desperately to keep up.
Galloping through fearful grounds,
One wrong step with the potential for death.

Jonathon Gatt (14)
Banff Academy, Banff

Acrid Smoke

Towering brick monsters,
Ever high in the doom-laden sky,
Shiny windows hidden,
No longer glisten in the sunlight.
No longer daylight,
Now deepening dark,
Dark as death.
Giant clouds of acrid smoke,
Dyed cancerous grey,
Spew from the skyscrapers,
Out and over rooftop car parks.
Brightly coloured cars,
Parked in anticipation.
Owners returning,
Hopefully soon, but unlikely.

Nicola Hadden (14)
Banff Academy, Banff

Endings

When the tune is finished
The song is sung
When winter is over
Spring has sprung
The words are said
When they've left your tongue
The debt is paid
When the deed is done.

Temptation is satisfied
When the hunger's fed
The tâpestry is finished
When there's no more thread
The adventure is over
When there's nowhere to tread
The soul is lost
When the man is dead.

Mhairi Anton (12)
Bell Baxter High School, Cupar

Fudge Doughnuts

Fudge doughnuts are my favourite food
They put me in a really good mood
To Fisher and Donaldson I must go
Even in the snow
If I do not get a fudge doughnut tonight
There is going to be a really big fight.

Fudge doughnuts are so creamy and delicious
I could eat loads, but my mum would get suspicious
I may get very fat
And look like a big prat
But who cares, fudge doughnuts are nice
Even if they are quite a price.

I wonder how many I could eat
Before I couldn't see my feet?
I think it would be quite a few
But I don't like waiting in that queue
Fudge doughnuts they really are the best
Better than all the rest.

Laurence Price (12)
Bell Baxter High School, Cupar

What Is Music?

Music is soft but loud
Music is unusual and proud
Music is short but long
Music is nothing but a song
Music is about love and care
Music is something to dare
Music is creative and fun
Music is the sound when spring has sprung
Music is something we cannot see
Music means so much to me.

Stacey Pover (13)
Bell Baxter High School, Cupar

Him

His eyes are like a trap
Luring you in closer
You look at them and can't stop staring
Without caring what the rest think
The wonderful green
The beautiful black
You never lose contact with them
Even if you never see him again
Even if you don't know him.

I know his eyes every time I see him
They float me away to Heaven
But there's one problem
I love him more than that
He's like my best friend but I do not know him
It's like I'm in a trap
And I can never be set free.

I love his smile too
He likes to smile in my direction
He likes to smile at me!
I don't know why
He just does.

His eyes
His smile
His name . . .

Alix Harvey (13)
Bell Baxter High School, Cupar

Domino

Domino, 'my cat'
A small lion cub
Curious of the big bad world
His pink baby rabbit nose twitching at new smells
His fluffy dog ears twisting in and out
To hear all the different sounds of life
His small beady eyes blinking at the sunlight
He looked around and he was ready for it all.

Domino, 'my cat'
A small lion cub
Was hungry
There was a rumble in his belly
And that was telling him he was a hungry cat
He was ready to catch his dinner
He would
Stalk his prey
Hunt his prey
And finally catch his prey!

Domino, 'my cat'
A small lion cub
But soon to grow up
Crept up my cotton desert bed covers
Not making a sound to be heard
His small beady whale eyes darted
He pounced on his helpless prey
With force of an elephant
He miaowed
It was a roar of a mighty lion
He was the king of the jungle.

Shannon Byrne (13)
Bell Baxter High School, Cupar

Life

Life was meant to be happy
But some people make it sad
By making wars and death and destruction
And making life feel really bad.

Third World countries, ill and dying
And parliaments in different countries badly lying
Why do people want destruction, violence and death
When we could all be happy?

With food, clothes and shelter
Everything a human being needs
With love all around them
And fulfilling their every need.

Catriona Dougall (12)
Boclair Academy, Bearsden

The Kestrel

A kestrel hovering
Is like a feather just floating
The kestrel just hovers
In the same spot waiting
Just waiting.

As its prey comes into its sights
It plunges from its heights
As it plunges with its talons spread
It grabs onto the mouse's head.

With a mouse in its talons
It takes it back to its nest
And feeds the baby kestrels
Again and again.

When the mature kestrels fledge
The cycle starts all over again.

Fraser Thomson (12)
Boclair Academy, Bearsden

Friends

Friends are important in every single way
They put a smile on your face
When you've had an awful day
You can tell them all your secrets
You can trust that they won't tell
They never ever lie even if you smell.

It's important to have friends
That will always be around
You can have a big sleepover
And play your favourite sounds
Friends will have your back
If there's something wrong
They know everything about you
Even your favourite song.

I have lots of friends
They make my life great
I couldn't live without friends
My life would be a state.

Hannah Lee (12)
Boclair Academy, Bearsden

The Ballerina

B allet is her life
A passion, a dream
L ong legs, straight back, a perfect bun
L eap, twirl, point your toes
E legant like a swan as she dances on a stage
R eady to go on, takes a deep breath
I nside herself are butterflies
N erves have kicked in
A ballerina just like me.

Jennifer Foley (13)
Bo'ness Academy, Bo'ness

Thud, I'm Down On The Ground

A year passes by
Thud, I'm down on the ground
Still I'm bullied
Thud, I'm down on the ground
Why do I walk these paths?
Thud, I'm down on the ground
For every day, they find me
Thud, I'm down on the ground
Verbally or physically they don't care
Thud, I'm down on the ground
As long as they hurt me they are happy
Thud, I'm down on the ground
Another year passes
Thud, I'm down on the ground
Then two years pass
Thud, I'm down on the ground
Well I've had enough
Thud . . . they are down on the ground!

James Smullen (12)
Bo'ness Academy, Bo'ness

Football

Left wing, right wing, front and centre,
It's almost time for the team to enter.
I'm puttin' on my football kit,
'Oh no, I've lost a fitba bit.'

The game has now begun
And everybody's having fun.
Someone's down; he's badly injured,
Dirty player, he'll see red!

The game is near its end
Will they be able to defend?
Oor number 10 he takes a shot
Will it go in or will it not?

Stuart Calder (12)
Bo'ness Academy, Bo'ness

Smoking

Dinni smoke, it makes you stink,
Dinni smoke, you'll look link a tink
I wouldni smoke if I wis you
You'll end up hingin ooer the loo.

You'll be in hospital and you dinni want that - do you?
I can tell you right now the food's no right
And I can tell you you'll be in a fight
I would be if they made me eat that
It's basically a lump of fat!

So dinni smoke, I'm warning you
You dinni want to land in hospital now, do you?

Megan Scotland (12)
Bo'ness Academy, Bo'ness

Horse Riding

Saddles, reins and jodhpurs too
All the things I bring for you.
Let's go trotting down the stream
I promise I won't make you scream.

Salsa, Secret and Tonto too
All the best are waiting for you
Even if you've fallen in the past
I promise I won't go too fast.

Cantering in every kind of weather
My God, this can't get any better
Go, go, go, right over the jump
I'm not surprised, my back's got a hump.

Rebecca Alexander (12)
Bo'ness Academy, Bo'ness

Joy

I am happy, I am great
I am fantastic and I'm never late!
I come for your Christmas, New Year and birthday
I go with people to church on Sunday.

If you're not happy then you are sad
In times like that there's no joy to be had.
But let me help your spirits to rise
Let me bring some joy to your eyes.

Everybody has joy some time in their life
I stretch from Edinburgh all the way to Fife!
But sometimes people don't see the fun
That there is to be had under the sun!

Conor Quigley (12)
Bo'ness Academy, Bo'ness

Shopping

Prada, Dolce & Gabbana
Buy them all - you know you wanna!
In and out the fancy shops
Buying all you can - never stop.

Going out in neat new clothes
It's a cure for all my woes.
In and out the fancy shops
Buying all you can - never stop!

Versace dresses and Liberana,
Going around eating some bananas
In and out the fancy shops
Buying all you can - never stop!

Katie Lourie (12)
Bo'ness Academy, Bo'ness

9/11

The fateful date, 9/11
A gleaming plane
Like an arrow, fired from Heaven
A boom, a crash, a shriek of pain.

A gaping hole in the tower,
The flames are now as tall as a man
The people within reaching their final hour
They try to escape if they can.

A man trapped in the fire's glow
Covered in cuts after the blast
In desperation jumped out the window
The sun hit his face, free at last.

Michael Preston (13)
Bo'ness Academy, Bo'ness

Happy Is . . .

Happy is the sun shining
Bright in the blue sky
Happy is the sun shining
It never makes you cry.

Happy is the birds singing
In the green trees
Happy is the birds singing
With great ease.

Happy is a rainbow
With colours red and blue
Happy is a rainbow
Which comes to see you.

Happy is the beach
With sand and shells
Happy is the beach
Just listen to the ice cream van bells!

Hannah Craig (12)
Bo'ness Academy, Bo'ness

It's Them!

It's them, they're coming
I hear them trying to find me.
'Come on wimp, show yourself
If you don't we will beat the life out of ya.'
It's late and dark so nobody will hear them beating me up.
Oh no, they are here and somebody can see me.
'There she is!' she shouts.
I scream and run; they follow close behind.
Soon they catch me and beat me up.
I wait until they are gone.
Then I pick myself up and do the daily walk home,
Limping with a busted nose
My mum is out so I go to my bed
Why do they do this?
Why do they care?
I'm just a person and I hate this nightmare!

Leighann Combe (12)
Bo'ness Academy, Bo'ness

Dust

As the cold wind swept the dust from the ground
We approached the chaos, silently not a sound
The smoke, the noise, the absolute destruction
Hardly one man stood strong among them
Men lay cold, drenched in a pool of red
All were once brave, now all are dead.

Then, a bang, a blast, all went numb
I fell to the ground, gasped, I was alone
But still all around me the slaughter went on
Bullet after bullet, flash after flash
Until all was gone, into the dust.

Alexander MacLeod (13)
Bo'ness Academy, Bo'ness

The Lauren And Natalie Poem

We were going to write a poem
Full of truth and glee
But the only topic we could find
Was on the subject of you and me.

I feel so happy
I feel so sad
But when we are together
Emotions can't be bad.

So let's dance around and sing
'Cause we are really sexy things
It's not that we're big-headed
It's just that we're connected!

Lauren Henderson & Natalie Mackay (15)
Bo'ness Academy, Bo'ness

Just Me

Here I am, this is me
This is my identity.
All I want is to be free,
Free to be who I want to be
Just me!

Here I am, this is me
Kind, quiet and quite dippy,
Green-eyed girl that's what they call me
Long hair, long legs, quite lanky
Just me!

Here I am, this is me
Rocker, rider and dancing queen
How lucky I am to have these
Friends and family who love me
For me
Just me!

Emily Fulton (12)
Bo'ness Academy, Bo'ness

The Girl

I would look at that girl often,
Her brown, curled locks of hair in the breeze,
Her feet tapping lightly down
On the wooden floor of the school hub.
If she looked back, I would often look down,
Feeling too shy to ask her.
And feeling embarrassed to think such things,
I had felt like this about other people,
But I was never appreciated back the same way . . .
. . . but she was different.

I would walk near that girl often,
As she passed, talking happily to her friends.
The aura around her felt warm, soothing,
Like being in the presence of an angel.
I feel for that beautiful girl, I really do,
But I couldn't let the feeling take over me again . . .
. . . the feeling of being let down again.
Other people always turned me down,
Because I was different . . .
. . . but she was better than this.

I saw that girl again today,
As she walked from the bus, talking with her friends.
She turned . . . and smiled . . .
. . . and waved at me . . .
I suddenly went warm,
With my friends sniggering at my brightened face.
This time, I dared not turn away,
But gave a small wave back, with a smile to match.
Maybe next time, I would think often
Maybe next time, we'll talk.

David Duncan (16)
Bo'ness Academy, Bo'ness

Nightmare

My dream was vicious and after several tries
I finally woke up with tears in my eyes.
For in this dream, lay the depths of Hell
Always too horrid for me to tell
But for everything there's a first, that's what they say
Waking up to nothing, just mist and grey.
The path was never-ending, nowhere to go
I wished I could wake up and just be at home.
The next thing I saw gave me loss of breath,
A gravestone stating my name and time of death
This couldn't be happening; no one else was here
And then one by one they started to appear.
Empty spirits, a gravestone for each one
None that would listen, I just wanted to know what was going on.
They all stood still, once again began to move
And for some strange reason, I knew what to do.
I sat at the side, next to my name
One after another they all did the same.
I started to shake as the thorns pushed through the dust,
As sharp knives, the colour of rust
They crawled up my legs and latched onto my arms
A piercing pain, leaving future scars.
But still no blood, as they tightened their grip
I tried to pull away, but they wouldn't let slip.
The pain was explicit and although it didn't seem
My nightmare was over; it was all just a dream.

Bronwen Winter (13)
Bo'ness Academy, Bo'ness

Wolf's First Winter

Small blue eyes look up as a cold nose
Is pushed into its fur, followed by a tongue
Yelping in protest, the wolf cub scrambles away
On oversized paws as its mother stays where she lays.

Its ears swivel forwards as eyes widen
When the wolf sees only whiteness outside
Cold, frosty, sparkling with tree branches laden
But though this happens for several months every year -
The wolf looks in awe, snuffling the cold air
For this is its first winter and it yelps in curiosity without care.

With an encouraging huff from its mother
The cub takes a careful step out of the den
And places a paw upon crisp snow
Squealing in fright at the cold before scrambling backwards, tail low.

Instant warmth surrounds the wolf as its mother approaches -
And she steps out of the den into the frost
Turning around to show her cub
And with an excited yap, the young wolf
Bounds out into the white world.

Bethany Winter (15)
Bo'ness Academy, Bo'ness

Dancing

D ance when you move to the beat
A movement is when you move your feet
N othing can stop you from singing along
C atching rhyme from that new song
I n the mood
N ow, you should
G et together and dance.

Sarah Finlay (13)
Bo'ness Academy, Bo'ness

The Tree

Deep within the ground below
It stirs, it wakens, it starts to grow.
From a tiny seed the shoot has sprung
Its fight for life has now begun.

From the forest floor it makes no sound,
Striving to leave its home in the ground.
The sapling trunk is supple yet strong,
It dances to the forest's song.

Stronger and stronger it gently weaves,
Pushing higher its bright green leaves.
The hole in the canopy it's aiming for
It just needs to grow a few feet more.

Finally, as high as it can go,
The canopy's leaves like a river flow.
For the tiny seed that struggled to be free,
Has now become a mighty tree.

Zoe Sayers (13)
Bo'ness Academy, Bo'ness

The Squished Spider

S neaking, silently, scuttling, searching, scared
P leading for mercy, wanted freedom
I nsignificant, anonymous, intrigued
D esperately dodging, diving the dangerous dog
E rm . . . almost there on the edge of the door
R eaching safety
S quashed on the step.

Kevin Reid (14)
Bo'ness Academy, Bo'ness

Alone

An empty room
An open door
There lay his body
But it wasn't her fault
Self defence, self defence.

An empty room
Empty but for the steaming iron
Looking guilty in the corner
He lay there also dead! Dying?
But it wasn't her fault
Self defence, self defence.

An empty room, empty
But for the fear
Should she turn herself in?
It wasn't her fault
He pushed her too far
He pushed her too far . . .

An empty room
She sat alone on the cell floor
Counting, counting
The years left on her sentence
But it wasn't her fault
Self defence.

Lauren Snedden (13)
Bo'ness Academy, Bo'ness

The Alien

He came from outer space
A creature from the unknown
Three eyes upon his face
From his mouth a groan.

He was a funny colour
A sort of greeny-blue
On one foot was a gutty
On the other was a shoe.

His head was very rounded
A football in disguise
A set of purple false teeth
Red streaks through his eyes.

His arms were long and skinny
His legs the very same
A funny sort of fellow
Nine toes or maybe ten.

Then there was a loud noise
It sounded like a crash
And then to my amazement
He was gone in just a flash.

Taylor McIntyre (13)
Bo'ness Academy, Bo'ness

Paranormal Discovery

The excitement rushed over her
She gasped with delight
Another discovery made
By the explorer and flashlight.

She's travelled the world, seen every sight
But never seen something like this
How is it possible in this lonesome cave
To find something so clear and bright?

The words stand out, written on the walls
A poem, story and riddle
All these curvy fancy letters
Muddled together in a strange messy fiddle.

She recognises this place, she's been here before
In a dream or maybe a song
She knows these phrases, heard them in her mind
She starts to feel this is wrong.

These words are worn, torn and shattered
They've been here for years and years
They describe this explorer, from inside to out
With all her dreams and fears.

Her heart's in her throat, she begins to scream
She can't take anymore
She runs away from this phenomenal sight
To be forgotten, for evermore . . .

Hannah Rose (13)
Bo'ness Academy, Bo'ness

This Poem Was Hard To Write

I couldn't write a poem, couldn't find the time
I couldn't write a poem, couldn't make it rhyme
But when I did, I couldn't stop it
I wanted my poem to be a hit
Bang! On the table came my fist.
'I can't write a poem,' I hissed.
I had rhymed but I could no more
Out of ideas I reached for the door
But suddenly it came to me
As if by magic an epiphany!
I would write on something I knew
About being unable to write a poem, that's what I'd do
The words came to me and I wrote it
This very poem, I chose to submit.

Rebekah Smart (13)
Bo'ness Academy, Bo'ness

How To Make A Rat

You need . . .
Eyes like cold spots staring at you and burning your skin
A snout as long and brown as a witch's broom
Teeth like silver needles sharp as a shark's senses
Ears with hearing like an owl that can hear a mouse a mile off
Whiskers threatening like a poisonous snake lying over your heart
Claws, deadly as the king cobra's bite
Fur, sticky like a young boy's mouth
A tail like a whip used by Indiana Jones
Shake them all together
Count to thirteen and there's your rat.

Sam Laurenson (13)
Brae High School, Brae

Confusion

A mixed up world where nothing makes sense
Where pictures, colours and sound collide into a flustered mess
A place where the sky is green and the grass is blue
The muffled wail in a crowd of turmoil
When even the bravest warrior breaks down in disorientation
As if there was a curtain between you and wisdom
The ballad of confusion.

Martha Morton (12)
Brae High School, Brae

Boredom

As bored as watching the sun go by
Watching drips of water falling from the tap
Sitting in silence as time goes slowly by
Looking outside the window staring deeply into the sky
As still as if nothing was ever there.

Josie Leask (12)
Brae High School, Brae

Guilt

A whisper as the tension grows
The sadness fills the quiet room
The pounding rain like teardrops falling
An empty smile as your mind churns
Twists of a deepening anger
The consequences of one mistake
The sharp fall of your freedom
Frayed knots as you try to escape
The cry of guilt comes from within
And defeat as the truth approaches
Come what may.

Rowan Johnson (12)
Brae High School, Brae

Words Of Sorrow

Sorrow is when I am alone and no one wants to call my phone
Sorrow is so slow, why doesn't it shoot me with a bow?
Sorrow makes me feel so small, I think I am going to fall
Sorrow makes me want to scream, it is not what it seems
Sorrow makes me feel hurt, my blood feels like dirt
Sorrow makes me want to burst, I think I am cursed.

Becky Rees (13)
Brae High School, Brae

Rainy Days

Dark and gloomy days
Long and sleepless nights
I lie awake, unable to sleep
Because of the pattering
Of the rain on the window
The next morning dragging on
An awful start to another day
I sit alone in the silent room
Every noise echoed
Sounds repeated
Drops of water
Made with hatred
Making the world miserable
Changing it to darkness
It disheartens us
Into the world below
And sinks us all
Into a great depression
Waiting for some light
To appear behind the dark clouds
Watching the time go by
Awaiting some sunlight
Hoping never to see
This disaster ever again!

Laura Hunter (14)
Broughton High School, Edinburgh

Guantanamo Bay

Here I am in Guantanamo Bay
Watching the birds fly away
What did I do wrong?
I must say

Here I am in Guantanamo Bay
Watching the birds fly away
Masks on
And about to pray

Here I am in Guantanamo Bay
Watching the birds fly away
There's nowhere to go
Nowhere to escape

Here I am in Guantanamo Bay
Wondering how life would be
Out of this place . . .

Zainab Hussain (14)
Broughton High School, Edinburgh

Ode To James

You are the anchor that steadies my boat of undying love
You are the ground beneath my feet
You are the sun that lights up my day
You are the wings that give my soul license to soar
I love the way you smile, it's erm . . . really nice
Yeah, so you're a mate.

Fergus Cook (14)
Broughton High School, Edinburgh

Water

It drips from your taps
It falls from the sky
And for those unhappy
It may gush from their eyes
Like a river
Dripping, gushing, flowing, streaming.

With it we are alive
Without it we would not survive
So when you see showers or rain
Do not stop and think, what a shame
Because without it you would not be here.

Without water there would be no
Dripping, gushing, flowing, streaming
Without water there would be no life.

Anja Campbell-McConnachie (14)
Broughton High School, Edinburgh

The Ice . . .

The ice, its smooth yet sinister shine
The cracks are appearing, line by line
As cold as the air when friendships are lost
And as wet as all the tears
It starts as rain, as snow, a storm
But ends in a puddle, not quite so warm
It lasts through the evening
And all the night
Before disappearing
In the afternoon light.

Gina Cameron (13)
Broughton High School, Edinburgh

In The City

I can see city lights but not much else
I'll stay right here, don't need your help.

Mummy never loved her and Daddy was a whore
Left home at fourteen, life became a bore.

Sells her body for money now, but still she has her soul
Goes home and chain-smokes, lungs as black as coal.

Immersed in obscure art and the poetry of romantics
Hidden under the covers, protection on the Devil's antics.

A day in the city is like a day in Hell
But still she loves it so
Sitting by the window at night, transfixed
By the non-stop traffic's glow.

Alice Bremner Watt (15)
Broughton High School, Edinburgh

Porcelain Doll

She lives on the floor
She cannot move
Her heart beats so fast
She's out of breath
A scared little angel, as bright as a star
Broken by a darkness behind a mask of love
Hiding in the corner, pretty little thing
But I just watch, unable to stop him
I will soon be broken too
Porcelain doll in the bin.

Rebecca Black (14)
Broughton High School, Edinburgh

The Tree

It represents life standing tall and proud
Its bare dark branches taking different directions
Some leading to dead ends, others to treasures
Some branches are smooth while others are rough
Like journeys we face in life
The path we choose determines the outcome.

The years go by, the roots grow stronger
Delving deep becoming one with the soil
Representing our growing, changing relationships
With family and friends
The bonds we form throughout the years.

As time goes by the tree matures
Providing shelter and protection to birds and insects
Witnessing births, nurturing creatures
We all hope we are kind, caring and protecting
It represents life standing tall and proud.

Alan Troake (14)
Broughton High School, Edinburgh

Choir

Like a bird they sing so well,
But on their own they go to Hell,
Just like thrushes they're here then gone,
But we'll never forget their wonderful song.

They're like eagles staring us out,
But as a budgie they have no doubt,
As they sing another song,
We all hope they'll carry on.

Ewan Zuckert (14)
Broughton High School, Edinburgh

The Abused Cat

In the shadows of the street corners you wait
Remaining mysterious as you prowl around
Looking for somewhere to rest
Although you have a home and a family
Returning home seems worse than anything else
Because there you are only neglected and abused
No animal should ever be treated like an object owned by humans
You feel like a ship caught in a storm
And trapped within your own reality
You must escape.

Andrew Vernon (14)
Broughton High School, Edinburgh

Senseless

Even though I can't tell you,
This problem does include a coo.
Actually, it's a coo times two
But it also includes a loo.

Therefore, here is my strife,
The coo did use this loo
And in the use of this loo
Took a life.

In what, though, is unknown,
The site where this extremity was blown
Creation can't create it
And evolution can't change it.

Calum Macleod (15)
Broughton High School, Edinburgh

Everywhere Are Clocks . . .

Everywhere are clocks . . .
Timers turn leaves
Tell birds to take off
Fish to return home
Restore desire
Shift scenery in the night sky
Lions and fish, crabs and birds
Move to the music of the moons
As we, too, dance to symphonies
Unheard. The year is a melody
We sing our lives in harmony
With singers invisible, yet magical
Fellow musicians whom we love
But do not know
The air is alive with chimes
Which summon us to celebrations
At which we feast on tears of happiness!

Rosie Shillinglaw (14)
Broughton High School, Edinburgh

Out The Classroom Window

Out my classroom window there is moss upon the school roof
The skivers sneaking back to school, all smoked out
There are nice green trees
And minted houses alongside Inverleith Park
St Steven's Street church ringing, *ding, dong, dang*
Princess Street in the distance
There is the mound, the galleries
And not forgetting Edinburgh's pride
The castle, high upon Castle Rock showing its
Glory!

Clarke Veitch (14)
Broughton High School, Edinburgh

Thoughts At Sea

The sun was burning high in the sky,
Reflection its rays upon the sea,
All the sailors ask themselves why
Why does the sea make you feel so alive?
And the answer was right in front all along
It gives you the power and the strength to thrive on.

Kelsie Stevenson (14)
Broughton High School, Edinburgh

Silent Witness

With a slap to the face
She falls to the ground
But the girl just stands staring
Without any sound
The tears are still streaming
Right down to her toes
But she dare not say a thing
Just keep it in close
She turns on her heels
I feel her just shudder
Thank God he's in bed
Her dear little brother
As she holds me so tight
I can't help but think
Why is it legal?
Why can he drink?
The sound of his voice
Just fills me with anger
But the words I can't say
For I am just a small tiger.

Amanda Laurenson (14)
Broughton High School, Edinburgh

?

Is there nothing more I can do?
Nothing more I can say?
To stop you leaving and turning away
From me, from us
Without you, I can feel this loneliness growing
It's swallowing me
Were you scared?
Were you angry?
Were you in pain?
And I was the bane of your existence?
Something changed . . .
In you, in me, in us . . .
Please let me in
Just a wee bit
Let me get to know you
And you can get to know me
Again and again . . .

Jordan McKenzie (14)
Broughton High School, Edinburgh

Wren

As I look out my window
On a cold winter's night
I see an old oak tree
Vaguely in sight
And up on this oak tree
A nest with some eggs
That will one day hatch
And have two legs
So when it grows up
And it's spring again
It flies off to freedom
That beautiful wren.

Jodie Robertson (14)
Broughton High School, Edinburgh

The Power Of Love

He loves me
I cry tears of joy
In a state of ecstasy
We're in love, me and my boy.

He loves me not
I cry tears of sorrow
We were in love or so I thought
My heart will be healed tomorrow.

He loves me
I cry tears of happiness
He's all I want him to be
We're in love, no more loneliness.

He loves me not
I cry tears of pain
We were in love or so I thought
The magic is lost once again.

He loves me
No more do I cry
An everlasting love for all to see
We're in love, see my heart fly.

Claire Ross (14)
Broughton High School, Edinburgh

The German Blitz

The petrifying sound of the Blitz siren screeches through the air
I feel a shiver down my spine as I think, *life's so unfair*
Everywhere I look panic has been sowing
As I hear a whistle blowing

I rush to the busy Underground
And think, *it's like being buried in a concrete mound*
It's so cramped, full of people trying to sleep
There isn't even enough room to sleep

The first wave of catastrophic bombs rains down on the city
I think of the people who have been bombed with pity
I thought of the bombs unemotionally falling
To kill anybody out calling

A deathly silence fills the Underground
You cannot hear any single sound
My ears are still ringing
But no one is singing

The welcoming sound of the safety siren fills the air
I should be happy, I know, but I have a care we all share
I feel my safety increased
As I know the bombing has ceased

I see soldiers and the Home Guard
Walking through buildings marred
I smell bodies who lived in the past
But I know I am safe at last.

Andrew McClement (12)
Campbeltown Grammar School, Campbeltown

The Abyss

A cocktail bomb whizzed past my head
I stalled then whirled around
While people fell to pieces
With a terrifying sound

A woman screamed from way within
Sent shivers down my spine
Before the darkness ate her up
And she snapped like thin pale pine

The creature down below
Was until now an enigma
But now will surely be the root
Of a united stigma

Against the very government
Who thought that it was fine
To just ignore, forget about
The staggering incline

For it was a hole that spanned a town
That tore from deep within
And once the people gathered round
You'd have heard a dropping pin

And now with riots breaking
At a single, tiny mention
The government, from whence they stemmed
Had finally caught attention

So now it's up to you my son
To carry on my voice
To banish all beneath the ground
And then we will rejoice . . .

Sam Glover (12)
Campbeltown Grammar School, Campbeltown

If I Could Change The Universe

If I could change the universe
The world would be a better place
Everyone would live together
No matter religion or race

There would be plenty of food and water
Enough for everyone
Clothes to suit all kinds of weather
A place to call our home

All animals and people equal
No suffering in our lives
No weapons of destruction
No bombs, no guns, no knives

No loneliness to think of
No sadness in our eyes
Just happiness and lovely thoughts
Where nothing at all ever dies

The grass would grow much greener
The trees would grow so tall
The flowers, beautiful colours
A much better place for all

If I could change the universe
The stars would come down to me
They would sparkle all around the world
For everyone to see
My world would be very different
A peaceful play to stay
If I could change the universe
If I had my own way.

Eilish Robertson (13)
Castlebay Community School, Castlebay

Nothing, Something, Everything, Anything

Nothing
For nothing it is quite big
It fills all emptiness
So it would be something.

Something
It can be something
Or something else
So it would be everything.

Everything
It is all somethings
But not nothings
So it would be anything.

Anything
If it isn't anything
It's something
But not everything.

Michael Gillies (13)
Castlebay Community School, Castlebay

Street Kid

Street kid
Full of fear
Once as strong as a lion
Now as weak as a mouse

No loving family to care for me
Left lonely in streets
Not even a warm bed
To sleep at night

Death seems near
To this young child
Street kid
Full of fear.

Rebecca MacLean (13)
Castlebay Community School, Castlebay

Orphan

I'm all alone
In the home
No mum, dad
Or mobile phone

I'm thirteen years old
I'm freezing cold
I desperately need
A caring soul

The carers say it'll be OK
But they say that day after day
Mummy left me when I was one
Decided to live her life in the sun

Day and night
I sit in fright
So lonely
No one in sight

But maybe some day
If I pray
Someone will rescue me
A new home to stay.

Marion MacLeod (13)
Castlebay Community School, Castlebay

Eye Of The Storm

The Caribbean sun -
The warming, welcoming glow,
Shines from up above.

Barbados ahead:
Visible from through the clouds,
We're about to land.

Sea and sand for weeks,
The only care is sunburn,
That is what I thought.

Looking at the sky
A storm is brewing above,
The clouds turning black.

No shelter too strong,
The hurricane could kill us,
Darkness up ahead.

Terrifying noise -
The wind whistling through the air,
The world seems to stop.

The eye of the storm,
Fear is running through my veins,
Silence is the worst.

Storm is over now
I can see the sunshine,
Until I look down.

Torment all around;
People crying, houses gone,
Could this be the end?

Michael Smith (14)
Craigie High School, Dundee

The Stirrers

They hear of a fight
And gallop over to watch
And enjoy the scene.

They stir up trouble
Just cause a reaction
Laughing innocently.

Spreading a rumour
They create a commotion
And smile with glee.

Known as The Stirrers
In school they are infamous
For their mischievous deeds.

They are animals:
Vultures scavenging for prey;
Hungry lions on the prowl.

With big blue eyes of ice
That analyse you in a fight:
Criticising your strength.

In appearance
They look like you and me,
But below they are dangerous.

Silently they plot
Their next disaster for you,
Just because you said something wrong.

After life at school
Society deals with them
They become today's criminals.

Heather Ellis (14)
Craigie High School, Dundee

The Pen

It sits cushioned between my fingertips,
Slow movements, flowing
As it forms the letters of the words
Encouraged by a simple mechanism
Its gentle tip touching the paper
Which in turn is no obstacle to cross

The pen has a mind of its own
A portion of knowledge at each drop of ink
Creating big or small letters
Using different fonts

But the colour of the pen doesn't change
It remains the subtle blue
The ink lying lifeless
As calm on paper as in real life

My hand motivates the pen
Allowing the words to materialise before my eyes
Its plastic covering disguising the power
Showing nothing special
After all, it's just an ordinary writing implement
Just an ordinary pen.

Erin Thomson (14)
Craigie High School, Dundee

School Bully

Ryan's in second year
He shoves little kids about
And makes them miserable.

Ryan hangs around
At the end of the school day
He's afraid to go home.

Ryan's dad often drinks lots
And is cruel and hits him
He doesn't care for Ryan.

So Ryan takes it out
On younger children
When all he needs
Is a helping hand
If anyone is brave enough
To offer it.

Cara Devereux (11)
Craigie High School, Dundee

Crash, Bang, Wallop!

I had mixed emotions
As that shiver ran down my spine
The thought of going to casualty
I was petrified

I was shaking
I was breathless trying to tell my story
I couldn't speak for a change
I was terrified

I was only going into the loft
Until I stood on the last rung
My world came crashing down
And so did I

The pain seemed so small
Compared to the shock and fear
Nothing prepared me
For that day

I broke a lampshade
With the thumping of my body
But most importantly I never wore socks
On the ladders again

For a while
I didn't go back into the loft
The memories just came pounding back
But look forward, not back.

Daryl Pattie (13)
Dumfries Academy, Dumfries

Ornithophobia

Black seas of tarmac, where giant monsters lie in wait.
Great birds of prey, looming over the queues of happy tourists.
Proud creatures of metal, wings outstretched,
And a great yawning hole where the eager people enter,
Enter to be consumed.

Clutching my bag like life's last breath
In the great ocean of the airport.
All alone, caught by the currents of people,
Then snatched back by the indifferent member of cabin crew,
A clone who leads me to the monster.

Brought forth to the stairs, up to what awaits.
Each step counts, each step brings me closer.
A hurricane hits from the great spinning teeth.
Now diving for the darkness to escape those huge propellers,
To more clones waiting.

Greeted with plastic smiles and sickly sweet voices.
Led down the aisle to a little blue seat.
They buckle me into the belly of the beast
And leave me there to ponder my fate,
Now all I have to do is wait for take-off . . .

Charlotte Singleton (13)
Dumfries Academy, Dumfries

Bhoys At First Sight

I can't believe I had won
Only at six it was still done
This would be excellent fun
To see the Bhoys
All of the waiting had come
Now all the joys

There lay dear ol' Paradise
Supporters running like mice
The feeling I had was nice
As players rolled in
The chill down my neck like ice
They had to win

One in, two in, three in, four
Five in, six in, seven in, more
This for sure was not a bore
Dons wiped away
I couldn't believe the score
What a great day!

Liam Pattie (15)
Dumfries Academy, Dumfries

The Sound Of Silence

Silent
As a cemetery
Cold, dull
The unspeaking children
The teacher pacing the aisles
The clock ticks but doesn't move
Silent
Not even a whisper
Scribbling pens
On crinkled paper
Row upon row
Of robot children
Movement is non-existent
Cars come and go
The green leaves fall
All
In
Silence.

Gemma Furlong (15)
Dumfries Academy, Dumfries

All Kinds Of Weathers

Snow, snow just like from an ice age
Twisting all over us
Snow is freezing cold
It is white and wet
You pick it up and it is squidgy
You can make a snowman or throw snowballs.

The sun shines all over the world
It gives us suntans, heat and light
The sun brightens everything up.

Rain is wet
It makes puddles and you need to wear
Waterproof jackets and wellington boots
Rain soaks you through.
Rain is good
It gives us drink and waters the plants.

Ross Johnstone (12)
Firpark School, Motherwell

Penalty

As you put the ball on the spot
You don't know if you'll miss or not.

The wind, blowing gently in your hair
The thought of missing you can't bear.

The weight of the supporters on your shoulders
It feels like a ton of boulders.

As you run up to take the kick
You feel as if you might be sick.

If you score the fans will roar
If you don't they will groan.

As your foot strikes the ball
It's in the net, well done from all.

Calum Wishart (12)
Gleniffer High School, Paisley

Day And Night

The clock chimes 12 o'clock
It's morning again
The sun bats the moon out of the sky
And takes to the stage
The full sky has been lit up
By the glittery belt of the sun
The moon is moody and is still
Drowning out of sight behind the trees
He is sneaking back up,
But he is too tired
And the sun is too bright for him
The sun has won her battle.

Sofie Graham (13)
Gleniffer High School, Paisley

The Free-Kick

Before it all started,
I knew it would happen,
Something special I thought,
Something special was to happen.

Two minutes in,
Twenty-five yards out,
He put the ball down,
Then like a hawk, he looked about.

Three paces back
He made sure the ball was right,
Thud, went my heart
Whack, what a strike.

It was curling and whirling
As fast as a bullet from a gun,
It hit the back of the net
And boy the crowd was stunned.

Kyle Cumming (12)
Gleniffer High School, Paisley

Young Writers - Away With Words Scotland

My PS2

When I'm on my PS2 I lose all track of time
I feel as if I'm part of the game
When I fail to complete a task, I smile and say it's OK
I'm really wearing a mask
Because I'm oh so sad, it makes me feel quite bad

I press reset and start again
I write down cheats with my lucky pen
My heart beats fast
I start to sweat
This is the best game
I've played yet
Yes, I've won
Happy days!

Fraser Murphy (12)
Gleniffer High School, Paisley

My PSP

I own a Sony PSP
It's a games console
It means a lot to me
I can listen to music
Play games too
Even watch a movie
As I lie tucked up cosy
Under my duvet
The screen is clear
The graphics are good
When I play my PSP
It lightens my mood
When bedtime calls
And it's time for sleep
I switch off my PSP
Put my head on my pillow
And begin to weep!

Ross Wylie (12)
Gleniffer High School, Paisley

Through Another's Eyes

I have known the feeling of being different,
I've felt the sadness of not being able to do some things.
Ride a bike, go up stairs . . .
I am lonely being the only one in a wheelchair, the only one that
Has to literally look up at everyone all the time.

And I have seen some people in a huddle, talking about the way I look
and act.

The multiplication of emotions: happiness, sadness and lack of
Confidence are the strongest emotions for me
Although pride is the most important.

I have heard the calming words of my family
They are more helpful than the words of a person
Who is paid to help people with their problems
I think through long afternoons of crying
And wondering,
Why me?

I should learn to keep my head up high and realise that they are
Just words!

After all we *are* all humans
We are *all* the same.

Lauren Gordon (12)
Gleniffer High School, Paisley

School

As I walk off the bus to hear
The sound of children laughing and having fun
Only for a few moments
As the school bell rings and the laughs turn to disappointment
We walk to class through the busy corridors thinking of the despair
that lies ahead

What more can I say, it's all work and no play
It might not be fun but better in the long run.

Lindsay Graham (12)
Gleniffer High School, Paisley

Who Am I?

I earn lots of lots of dosh
And have a pretty wife called Posh.

Brooklyn and Romeo my two little boys
I love to play with them and their toys.

I have a very successful career,
That lets me model some trendy gear.

To illustrate my flare and passion,
I do keep up with the latest fashion.

Real Madrid was once my team
American football is now my dream.

To LA I travel far,
To a team that sounds like a candy bar.

LA Galaxy here I come,
Let's kick the ball and have some fun.

David Beckham is my name,
Playing football is my game.

Dawn Thompson (12)
Gleniffer High School, Paisley

The Photo Frame

I hold memories of pretty faces
Proud moments and some of despair
Comic smiles and dressed up children
But now there is tension in the air
The divorce just came through
The children have left
And I am forgotten at once
Where is the family I used to show off?
They have gone and my photos are not worth tuppence.

Aisling Gilbert (13)
Gleniffer High School, Paisley

A Walk Through The Night

A young girl went for a walk at night,
All alone, with no one in sight.
She walked through an empty park,
She couldn't see anything, it was so dark.
Suddenly a noise came from behind,
But she thought it was nothing, only her mind.
She carried on walking down the path,
Now very scared, this was no longer a laugh.
But just as she was about to go out,
She heard someone start to shout.
Her heart began to pound very fast,
She didn't know what to do; she just froze on the grass.
But things are not as they seem,
Soon she woke up, it was only a dream!

Louise Conn (13)
Gleniffer High School, Paisley

Lenny The Dog

I'm Lenny the lazy dog
I lie around and sleep like a log
I have big brown eyes
I like chasing flies
I have floppy ears
I don't have a lot of fears
I love running around and fetching my ball
I'm not a small dog, but I'm not very tall
I have a bone-shaped name tag
If I'm happy my tail will wag
I'm given lots of bones to chew
If you give me a pat I'm sure to love you
I love going to the beach and swimming in the sea
One thing I know is . . .
Not many dogs are as happy as me!

Lyndsay Hamilton (13)
Gleniffer High School, Paisley

Why Do They Stop And Stare?

Why do they stop and stare at me
Why is it they cannot see?
I am a child just like them
Living and breathing, I'm just the same.

I like to play outside and in
Carry on and make a din
Just because I'm in a chair
Doesn't mean they can stop and stare.

Now music time is just a hoot
Guitar, keyboard and trumpets toot
Drum beats, violins, double bass, sax
Are easy for me, that's a fact.

I'm just the same
Why can't they see
I'd love to climb and fall from a tree
Chase a butterfly or honeybee.

Drive a car or ride a bike
Get into trouble for being a tike
This is normal, I have to share
It's just the same being in a chair.

Skiing down a slidy slope
For all this I live in hope
All these things I will do one day
And hope and hope that time will pay.

It's only my legs that do not act
So please stop staring and accept the fact
I am the same and want to be
Accepted for nothing, except being me!

Leigh Sweeney (12)
Gleniffer High School, Paisley

My Little Angel

My little angel watching over me,
My little angel will always be there,
Always looking after me,
With all her special love and care.

My little angel gives me hope,
She helps me get through the day,
Even when I'm down in the dumps,
Oh little angel what can I say.

Little angel, are you big
Or are you small and can you fall?
So many questions I would ask
If I could meet you, is it possible at all?

Little angel your love is endless,
How could I ever let you go?
Sorry for all the trouble I have caused,
Little angel I love you so.

Fiona Dickson (13)
Gleniffer High School, Paisley

Winter

Snowflakes falling on the ground
Glistening, sparkling
Whirling around.

Frozen water turns into ice
Slippery and hard
Not very nice.

Out in the cold with gloves and scarf
Running around
Having a laugh.

In the evenings sit by the fire
Feeding it wood
Making the flames higher.

Andrew Harper (13)
Gleniffer High School, Paisley

Night - Who's Out There?

When our country is at rest
And everything is quiet;
Who goes out there in the dark
To make sure we're OK?

When the hospital is busy
And the ambulance is away;
Who goes out there in the night
To make sure we're all safe?

When the police are solving cases
And the jail cells are all full;
Who goes our there in our country
To stop criminals getting away?

When the fire brigade is rushing
And everything is controlled;
Who goes out there in the dark
To try to save the day?

Although our country seems at rest
And everything is calm;
Somebody is out there
To keep us all away from harm.

Hannah Mawhinney (13)
Gleniffer High School, Paisley

Neds

Neds this, Neds that
Neds all in the news
All they ever do is
Smoke and drink strong booze.

'Won't yer go,'
One will say
Then punch you in the face
Then he'll cackle just a little,
'At'll put ye in yer place.'

I loathe these little wasters
That think they're actual mad
They're all just little jag bags
They're all terrorising ladies
And stealing their handbags
But all they really want
Is a lighter and some fags.

An ASBO is a medal
They show it off in pride
And when we see them down the street
All we can do is hide.

Colin Harper (13)
Gleniffer High School, Paisley

There's Plenty To Go Round

Springtime joys are here at last
The joys of life are all around
The winter winds have surely passed
Spring is here and there's plenty to go round.

Summertime comes waltzing in
The sun shines its light down
The heat and warmth are all around
Summer is here and there's plenty to go round.

Autumn leaves begin to fall
The life around begins to fade
The colours fade but will come again
Autumn is here and there's plenty to go round.

Winter winds have come again
Snow falls during the night
To arrive on frost-filled mornings
Winter is here and there is plenty to go round.

Greg Laird (13)
Gleniffer High School, Paisley

The Storm

The winter winds are howling
Although the sun spurts through the sky.

Wintertime is here
Now the summer months are gone by.

There's a distant sound of thunder
And a stillness in the air.

A sudden flash of lightning
Lights the sky up like a flare.

The sun peeps out from behind a cloud
And a rainbow fills the sky.

The dark clouds soon fade away
Now the thunderstorm has gone by.

Lindsay Campbell (13)
Gleniffer High School, Paisley

The Sea

Hydro and aqua
With roaring breakers and whispering ripples
Beneath the depths lie secrets and treasures
Yet to be discovered

It's a beautiful sight
Green and blue
The ambling current
The crashing waves
Smashing the coast
Like a hammer and nail

Out of the blue
Emerges a dark shape
A dolphin leaping about
How I'd love to be him

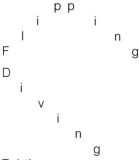

```
          p p
     i          i
   l                n
F                      g
D
   i
      v
         i
            n
               g
```

Twisting
Having fun

The sea
To be cherished
Always.

Nikola Zikic (13)
Gleniffer High School, Paisley

Being A Teenager

When you're a teenager it can be kind of tough
Squeezing spots makes your skin rough
Hormones are like traffic lights, changing all the time
Friends want to try things, whisky, beer and wine
Not me you see, I've got more brains
I'll stick with moods and body growing pains.

Since I went to high school, new people to impress
Everybody jockeying to see who's got the best
Best trainers, best clothes, North Face or Mera Peak
It's hard keeping up every day and every week.

New friends, girlfriends, emotions going wild
Mum and Dad asking, 'What's happened to our child?'
Hey, I don't know, but I know this
I need a tenner for fun at the flicks
Two quid for 'deo' to stop my BO
We're growing up, us kids.

Elliot Whitnall (12)
Gleniffer High School, Paisley

Summer Fun

Smiling down
The sun is singing
Its rays touch the ground.

A bee flies by
Smelling the flowers
It stops to say hi.

Animals go play in the water
Laughing and shouting
The weather grows hotter.

Just one cloud in the sky
Jumping about
As it floats by.

Longer days come
So the children play longer
They look for puddles, but there are none.

Sarah Semple (13)
Gleniffer High School, Paisley

Teenagers

Getting strange looks
If you wear a hoodie
Being branded by the same iron
Cheeky and moody.

Don't worry though
We're not that bad
And we're not in a mood with you
Sometimes we just get sad.

All the worries we have
Friends, cliques, school
Family, fitting in
Confidence, self-image, being cool.

Some say we all
Smoke and drink
Get into fights
Well, that's what they think.

OK, there are teens who
Terrorise their neighbourhood
Who roam the streets
Being crude.

But the majority of us
We're fine
We don't go too far
We know where to draw the line.

Fiona Gemmell (13)
Gleniffer High School, Paisley

Waiting

How long left? How long to go?
The girl behind keeps saying so.
Whilst the boy in front taps his feet,
To the most annoying little jazzy beat.

I look at my watch it's 12.33
It seems like forever, what's wrong with me?
It feels like I've been here for a day,
If I don't get served soon I'll be old and grey.

I fold my arms; I'm getting rather cross,
If I don't get served soon, I'll demand to see the boss.
But I don't want to cause a stir, I'll continue to wait,
Even if it means to wait until 4.48.

Finally the man in front has started to budge,
I thought he was stuck like hot sticky fudge.
I have moved quite a bit,
Perhaps some people in front have decided that's it.

I'm nearly there, I've reached a bend,
Perhaps this line will come to an end.
I take one look and start to whine,
It seems like I'll have to wait in another line!

Ainsley Miller (13)
Gleniffer High School, Paisley

My Other Senses

As I wake up in the morning
To the wonderful smell of toast
I sit up very gently
And suddenly hear the post

I feel the carpet touching my feet
I can hear the dog bark
I go down the stairs slowly
To get ready to go to the park

As I walk along the road
I can hear the cars drive past
And I think a few of them
Are going very fast

My dog he is very smart
He guides me through my life
He always knows when to stop and start
And saves me a lot of strife

As you might guess I am blind
But I still live my life to the full.

Andrew Baldacci (12)
Gleniffer High School, Paisley

She's Not Gone

She's standing here beside me
Her cold breath on my skin
I reach out for her hand
It's feeling very thin.

She's standing here beside me
Her scent circling my face
I breathe in another time
To keep the scent in case.

She's standing here beside me
Her voice whistling near
I listen, yet another time
It's free, it has no fear.

She's standing here beside me
I turn, I know her well
I look to find not her
But a picture for me to dwell.

She's standing here beside me
Not in person but in mind
Her pictures, voice, her scent
The only things I find.

Natalie Duncanson (13)
Gleniffer High School, Paisley

Life At Midnight

A life at midnight:
Blue just a four-letter word
In Braille beneath the fingers
Which have seen more life
Than the eyes designed to guide them.

Every sound an encyclopaedia;
Knowledge imparted by the
Groan of tired floorboards,
Under leather boots that creak
Or the soft whisper of silk slippers.
Each small song of symphony
Of raw emotion, bleeding into the air.

The scent of a rose a paradise
Enfolded in the damp velvet
Of trembling petals,
With no idea of redness to distort it.

What tragedy a life at midnight
When clear laughter tells a smile,
Cold roughness is the grating speech of stone
And roses smell sweeter in darkness?

Pippa Janssenswillen (16)
Gordonstoun School, Elgin

The Firebird

All is silent, still, subdued . . .
Darkness claims the night,
But in the dim, there is a spark,
A spark of life, of light.

An angry hiss out in the dark,
Angry at being roused,
Downy sparks fly from the gloom,
A fire that can't be doused.

An angry squawk, a puff of breath,
And then a silence again,
When all at once, a fearsome screech,
The firebird takes to wing.

Shooting into velvet heights,
A trail of stars behind,
Screeching out a deafening shriek,
Betraying its furious mind.

Shrieking, screaming, squealing, screeching,
Higher, higher he flies,
When all at once a mighty crack
And sparks rain from the skies.

A myriad of colours,
An explosion of rainbows,
A kaleidoscope of sparks and stars,
His bright plumage he shows.

With a final screech and haughty squawk,
The blinding colours die,
The brilliant feathers float to ground,
From the velvet sky.

And the firebird is silent, still, subdued.

Gail Fulton (16)
Greenock High School, Greenock

Fear Of The Holocaust

A group of dead bodies,
How did they get there?
Was it in a concentration camp,
Where a victim couldn't bear?

Jews had to wear yellow stars,
Wherever they may be.
Nazis steal expensive cars
Or whatever they could see.

If they're in a camp
They will soon die on the spot.
But if they don't abide
They will eventually get shot.

From abuse to murder,
It's a very big jump.
After a day or so,
The bodies smelled like a dump.

Women cut their fingers
And rubbed it on their face.
They did that so they could stay here,
Instead of a killer place.

Some say it was showers,
Some say something else.
It's gas chambers and they kill
And the place is diseased and smells.

He killed millions of people,
Some wonder why
Was it just the German party
Or the evil Austrian guy?

William McGeachy (14)
Greenock High School, Greenock

ACTIVboard

The cursor is moving but no one is near me
Low-tech teachers have always feared me
But blackboard and chalk are a thing of the past
The ACTIVboard is here to last

On training day drywipes go away
For the ACTIVpen and the docking bay
Some decent computers wouldn't go amiss
But when you request yours, you're at the bottom of the list

Number 13 is unlucky for some
But the room on B Floor seems to have won
HP Desktop 12993
Pentium 4 processor - always beats me

Mr Connell's been upset you see
Because his wee drywipe board is far too wee
He wishes he had his old blackboard back
But for media studies the projector's a whack

And now that technology's moving on
Mrs McCusker's doing nothing wrong
She's buying another ACTIVboard you see
And Miss Dick's the favourite for the new technology

But how will it work on this Windows 2K?
Is a new computer on its way?
Oh no, an IBM ThinkPad on the stands
When will they realise the flaw in their plans?

What a catastrophe - the ACTIVboard fail!
Now even Mr Anderson's is beginning to fail
But what can we do to improve our IT?
Watch and wait . . . watch and wait . . . watch and wait.

Joseph Craig (14)
Greenock High School, Greenock

Colours

Blue
Sky
Rain
Tears that now run down my cheeks.

Red
Blood
Rain that forever marks the floor
My hands as I move the blade and strike once more.

Green
Rebirth
Spring
New grown grass that is now growing over her grave
She meant a lot to me
But now and forever
She shall be the death of me.

White
Peacefulness
Snow
Surrounds my vision as finally I am free.

Free from betrayal
Free from death
Free from regret
Free as the day I was first born.

Elaine Willdridge (17)
Greenock High School, Greenock

Last Summer

Last summer I hated you, it's the truth we all know
Last summer I knew my hate would not fade
Last summer your life came apart in my hands
And I could not heal the scars I had made.

Turn back time, how I wish I could
Stop the clock and wind it back
Go back to last summer, if only I could
For now I miss the girl we all lack.

My insides boiled like a cauldron of death
The hate I first knew grew stronger each day
I detested your voice, your face and your clothes
You didn't know then the price you would pay.

Turn back time, if it's not too late
Oh, how I wish I knew the way
Go back to last summer, I know it's too late
But I told myself I would, some day.

Don't worry; of course I know who's to blame
You soon found out there was nowhere to hide
My words tied a noose around your neck
I watched as you struggled and laughed as you cried.

Turn back time, how I wish I could
Stop the clock and wind it back
Go back to last summer if only I could
For now I miss the girl we all lack.

Death occurs everywhere, every day
But I never knew how guilty I'd feel
For the girl I once hated, detested, lost
I want to change time, but some scars never heal.

Miriam Chappell (13)
Harris Academy, Dundee

Here Lies . . .

Here lies her stone
Visited by more than one
Here lies her self
Loved by everyone
Here lies her memory, her soul and her mind
There are the people that she left behind.

Weeping are her friends she was a happy soul
Once again now they'll never feel whole
There sits her sister, regretting every fight
Resenting the hate she felt almost every night
There are her parents watching the crowd go wild
Unaware of the fact that they hardly knew their child.

Here lies her stone
Awash with many tears
Here lies her self
A companion through the years
Here stand the few who knew the real girl
Who stood by her through all her struggles with the world.

The ones she longed to forgive without hate
Her child, her love, the one who'd wait
The one whose poison she'd gladly drink
The one who understood the way she'd think
The one with the power to heal her scars
The one who saved her from all the liars.

Here lies her stone
Still going strong
Here lies her self
Never been too wrong
Here lies the one who can no longer be
Here lies my memory and soul, here lies me.

Naushin Nawar (13)
Harris Academy, Dundee

Bottlenose Dolphin

You brethren of the nether sea
Who leap and play so happily
Singing songs amid the fish
Doing whatever you would wish
I wish I could, one day, meet you.

Most of the world does not like me
They use big nets and I have to flee
Tursiops Truncatus my given name
Always playing an endless game
Twixt the reefs and shores.

When we use those fishing nets
To catch fish for our fussy pets
We need to think of our dolphin friend
To keep him playing till his natural end
Forever leap the dolphin wild and free!

Susannah Cummins (13)
Harris Academy, Dundee

A Stormy Day

The grey clouds gather
The wind howls in anger
For a storm is breaking

The water ripples
People pile into their houses
Dogs strain at the leash

Trees bend in the wind
The baby cries in his pram
Yet the cat sleeps on.

Ewan Patterson (13)
Harris Academy, Dundee

The Firebird

A cigarette lies by the wooden stairs
Dropped by a man with no cares
On the carpet the colour of earth
Is the perfect place for a firebird's birth.

Within a second, without a sound
The firebird crawls upon the ground
As it stands, it stands tall
And lets out a whispering call.

Up the stairs the creature creeps
Up to helpless child who sleeps
Its feathers fall and scorch the floor
As it starts to burn her door.

The beast's fury as it screams
Wakes the child from her dreams
The firebird crashes into her room
She cowers awaiting her certain doom.

The firebird finally faces its prey
And for a second it will stay
But soon it plunges its burning beak
And sears the flesh on the child's cheek.

The water snake ends the beast's rage
Entwining it like a writhing cage
As the firebird screams in fright
The serpent ends its brutal flight.

As time goes on the firebird dies
Water dimming its glowing eyes
At the end all that's left
Is the firebird's victim and its breath.

Joanna Bone (13)
Harris Academy, Dundee

It's Not As Easy As It Looks

Every day you're getting older
And things start to change a lot
Suddenly you're not a child
Your childhood's starting to rot.

You're starting to feel angry
Suddenly getting mad
You can't seem to control yourself
And ruining the life you had.

The friends you had are going
New ones are coming in place
Everybody's going crazy
It's like a never-ending race.

Guys seem to become attractive
You begin to fall in love
You believe every word they say
You're floating like a dove.

Then suddenly life crashes
They say they want more
You don't know what to do
Even breathing becomes sore.

That's when it all becomes too much
And you look up to the sky and pray
Oh God, I beg of you take the pain away.

Ruqueia Ossman (13)
Harris Academy, Dundee

King Of Neds

(Ned: Non Educated Delinquent)

He feels tough as he walks
Like nothing and nobody can stop him
His followers like sheep surround him
Spurting words that only others of his kind understand.

He lights a cigarette taken from his dad
And the smoke flows up like snakes being charmed
The tracksuit he wears is no longer white
But the second fighter has more to worry about.

The smaller boy had been used like a punchbag
And had been left with his followers
Something deep inside challenged him to care
But he refused and washed away his troubles with alcohol.

Anyone who dares to be different will suffer
For in his ideal world everyone is like him
After all, he is popular, isn't that what matters?
'Outsiders' disgust him, what makes them so great?

They are all weak and edgy on their own
So they prefer to travel in packs
They are loud and abusive to anyone they meet
''Cause they're the best ya' ken?'

Hannah Kane (13)
Harris Academy, Dundee

Volcano

The Earth is shaking
Liquid fire seeping to the top
There isn't much time left

Just another day
Then in a pyre of ash and rock
Mountain wakes again

Too late to run now
You can only watch in horror
As the grey fire burns

There is no escape
You look your death in the eye
Cremation is quick

The trees are all dead
Walking on the moon on Earth
Mountain is silent

Soon the grass will grow
But for now all is at peace
Calm after a storm

Shadow of the hill
Turning paradise to hell
Now and forever.

Anna Grinev (13)
Harris Academy, Dundee

This Garden Of Lies

This garden of lies you've planted where the roots grow so deep
You sewed the seeds for it the moment I said hello
The insects and birds that land on the petals of heartache
Are blind to what they are resting on
They are the people around us
The ones who embrace this garden of lies.

The vegetable patch growing in the corner
Is your next harvest of tales
Which you will feed to the people
It will nourish them and keep them fed.

The fountain of stone is as cold as every sentence you weave
And you do it so gracefully like the spider at the other end of the lawn
Each blade of grass on that lawn stabs like the truth has now
The roses of love that seemed so fresh and real will wither away.

I wish I could trample them away
But the roses were so beautiful, they had grown so fine
I refuse to believe you ever planted a garden of lies
The roses I grew for you were true, I tended them every day to keep
them strong.

I wish you'd never planted a garden of lies and let the roots grow
so deep
I wish you'd never sewn a single seed
I wish you'd never had a single harvest of tales
This garden of lies where the roots grow oh so very deep.

Tara Matthews (13)
Harris Academy, Dundee

Dreams

Ever thought, when you sleep
A dragon, fairy you will met?
Deep down in your mind
A pleasant dream you hope to find.

Now close your eyes and count sheep
Slowly drowning until you sleep
What dreams come today?
Or maybe nothing to your dismay

Waking up from a dream
How disappointed you may seem
Can't wait until tonight
For my dream, isn't that right!

Sarra El-Wahed (13)
Harris Academy, Dundee

A Crushing World

They hurt me
I feel it inside
I'm like a bee
Waiting to die.

The lightning strikes
The thunder roars
They come on their bikes
In twos and fours.

They throw bricks
The smash is clear
They throw sticks
The pain creeps near.

They kick and punch
I want to break free
They steal all my lunch
I want to die.

Mhairi Fenton (13)
Harris Academy, Dundee

Fire

Fire is alive, popping and crackling
People inside in energy they're lacking
Blue, orange, yellow and red
They would never go to bed
Crack, hiss and whiplash
With a pop, bang and a bash
They talked in an unknown tongue
Sparks at each other they flung
The *hero* of them all
Has never had a fall
But he's a liar
He doesn't tire
And that's what's inside a *fire!*

Tom Walkinshaw (13)
Harris Academy, Dundee

A Hamster

A small timid creature
With tiny pink feet and claws
Wakes in the late afternoon light
To groom its silky pink paws.

He tiptoes while stretching
To his little bowl of food
Stuffs the pieces into his mouth
To enjoy the taste of good.

He scatters about the enclosed cage
Looking for a friend
But fails like a torn out page.

He wanders back to his warm little bed
Feeling lonely like an unwanted child
Because all he has is himself.

Sarah Menzies (13)
Harris Academy, Dundee

The Circus Elephant

I stand on the edge of the ball,
Keeping my balance so I cannot fall.

I'm so afraid of these watching eyes
I might fall over and hurt my beautiful thighs.

Holding their tomatoes ready to throw,
As I jump from the ball I hear a loud, 'Go!'

Covered in tomatoes, smelling of musk
They climb over my elephant tusks.

Have I lost my elegant touch?
Would I be the first elephant to use a giant crutch?

Isra Al-Saffar (14)
Harris Academy, Dundee

The Day And Night Of A Cat

Sunlight brightens everything it hits
The purring creature, sullen and sleek
Its evil eyes are narrow black slits
It makes a skilful jump from floor to wall
And looks around for new prey.

Moonlight brings in darkness
The purring feline, bulky and cute
Her bold eyes are filled with love and happiness
She lies around stretched out on carpet
And is satisfied with her day.

Hester Astell (13)
Harris Academy, Dundee

Am I Really That Dumb?

I have blonde hair
And lots of money
I live in Hollywood
But does that matter?

I set the trends
And walk on red carpets
I have cameras in my face
But does that matter?

Believe it or not
I'm a person too
I may not be clever
But does that matter?

Just because I'm famous
And go to movie premieres
People ask me for autographs
But does that matter?

People put me down
Because my daddy's rich
I'm in magazines
But does that matter?

I wish I had real friends
Who like me for who I am
I'm not really that dumb
Underneath I'm just like you.

Fiona Leslie (13)
Harris Academy, Dundee

Joey

Watching his kingdom
With great pride
Wings twitching
There's nowhere to hide.

Out of his cage
He does flutter
Surveys his land
Then rests near the butter.

Into his village
Comes a stranger
Panic strikes
He thinks he's in danger.

He takes off
But is stopped in mid-flight
It doesn't intend to hurt him
But is scared that it might.

In the stranger's gentle grasp
He is put where he belongs
His new home is colourful, energetic
It isn't as bad as he suspected.

From being alone, independent
To being cared for and loved
There was no doubt which life he liked best
He could get used to this.

Emily Spasic (13)
Harris Academy, Dundee

The Watchdog

The black shadow bides his time
Through the sleeping house he creeps
A mighty statue on his guard
Stalking a suspected thief.

A vague silhouette floats past the window
Swift with stealth the watchdog leaps
The door opens, a river of dim light flows in
Shining on his pearly teeth like pointed diamonds.

A coward flees into the night
No roar from the lion's den is made
He stands proud, above his defeated challenger
Once again he returns to stone.

Channelle Buchan (14)
Harris Academy, Dundee

Fishy Instincts

The lonely fish swam alone
In the endless ocean
How I'd love to be a man, thought he
Perhaps he should drink some potion.

He gathered some seaweed from the surface
And took a pearl from a sulky clam.
He got some shells then mixed them together
And took an enormous swig
His fin went funny, perhaps a little curly
Then he turned into a pig!

Jane Caird (13)
Harris Academy, Dundee

Rainy Day

Umbrellas open up like giant lollipops
Rain tumbling to the ground in tiny little drops
People rushing and squealing as they go
They all hate the rain, they wish that it was snow.

Birds awoken in their home-made nests
To a sound of water all around
A sound they do detest
They fly away to the dampened soil
To find the worms dead underground
Oh what a time of terrible toil!

I'm tumbling and spiralling down to the street
The others around me I'm trying to win
Then I smash into concrete with a terrible din!

Hayleigh Cameron (13)
Harris Academy, Dundee

The Eagle

Flying high above the hill
Looking for his daily fill
Soaring and swooping through the sky
Looking downwards with his eagle eye.

Swooping swiftly down to the ground
Silently descending without a sound
The rabbit dashes from left to right
Avoiding the eagle, staying out of sight.

The eagle's claws outstretched towards its prey
In a downwards thrust for its catch of the day
Upwards the eagle supreme in flight
Powerful and elegant in all its might.

Elaine Abbott (14)
Harris Academy, Dundee

Lightning

(Gary Numan, apart from being a popstar, has a pilot's licence)

Bang!
Goes the tree
In a flash of light
It falls
Cracking the earth beneath it
The lightning moves on
Flying
Just like Gary Numan.

Crash!
Goes the window
In a flash of light
It smashes
Cracking into one thousand pieces
Like dreams
Crushed by the Devil
As himself.

Eilidh Keith (13)
Harris Academy, Dundee

The Leopard

Her head is held high
As she claims her prize
Which took her a while to seize
She tried to hide in a bush
But it was too much of a shmoosh
So she decided to hide in the trees
She jumped down on her prey
And it didn't run away
So she knew at once she'd beaten it
It seemed very violent
But then it went silent
So then she decided to eat it.

Jennifer Glass (13)
Harris Academy, Dundee

The Eagle

From his castle in the sky, he perches upon his throne
Far above the earth he waits
Standing proud, surveying his kingdom
Watching, waiting for his prey, unsuspecting on the ground.

Powerful and strong the eagle remains
Cruel-eyed he scans his domain
Flexing his talons, getting ready to kill
He spots a young rabbit and flaps his wings.

He soars through the sky jolting this way and that
Following his victim through the undergrowth
Halting, hovering, playing his game
Before plummeting down to kill.

He grasps his prize with sharpened talons
It wriggles and squirms trying to break free
Ripping and tearing the eagle spills blood
Suddenly . . . all is still.

An eagle, a king, a killer.

Catriona McNeish (13)
Harris Academy, Dundee

The Eagle

The eagle soars through the sky
In a majestic way
Scanning the ground, bloodthirsty
Searching for his prey.

Suddenly he spots a rabbit
And plummets to the ground
He snatches the rabbit in his claws
It squeaks, then makes no sound.

Michaela Netto (13)
Harris Academy, Dundee

The Dolphin

The dolphin glides smoothly through the water
Surrounded by family and friends
Splash!
She draws a rainbow through the air
What a beautiful sight.

Click, click, click
The dolphin waits for a reply
Using teamwork she and her friends
Ambush helpless fish
Until her belly is full
What a beautiful sight.

The dolphin is hungry again
They start to chase once more
But the fish are already being hunted by a deadly thing
The net comes speeding along with no escape
What a terrible sight . . .

The net today is heavier to haul up
It is heaved onto the deck
The dolphin is dead
Her elegant lifeless body tangled in rope
What a terrible sight.

Carina MacDonald (13)
Harris Academy, Dundee

The Eagle

Golden king of clear blue sky
Searching with his beady eye
Should a rabbit he espy
Down to earth he'll dive.

Homing in upon his prey
Early morning, break of day
Spots a mouse from far away
Down to earth he'll dive.

With his talons sharp as steel
Sorry's not how he will feel
In his claws he has his meal
Down to earth he'll dive.

When he led the men of Rome
In their battles far from home
The battlefield for food he'd comb
Down to earth he'd dive.

On a cliff he'll build his nest
Lined with feathers from his chest
Hunger soon disturbs his rest
Down to earth he'll dive.

Freya Schofield (13)
Harris Academy, Dundee

Sardine

You are such a skinny malinky
You are so elegant
But really you're a bit minky
Other cats just think you're arrogant.

To your distaste you've been named after a fish
They say your name is Sardine
Pleading there sitting, your tail going swish
Waiting, waiting for anything.

You have no moral code: every moggy for itself
What you find is yours, no one can take it
Find a good home and you'll live in good health
By these and more if you abide, you can make it.

I do pity you locked in a cage
No one to love you, no one to care
In your frustration and in your rage
Waiting, waiting for anything.

Emily Ralston (13)
Harris Academy, Dundee

The House Next Door

One dark night I lay down to rest
I hear the TV blaring
But is there somebody staring?
I lay down to rest
I see the house, the house next door
See the grand oak door
I see creatures bumping about
But I have my doubts
I hear malevolent people screaming
But am I dreaming?
I woke up, I woke up
Isn't silence golden?

Gwyn Jones (12)
Holywell High School, Holywell

The Anger Of War

It starts as soon as day becomes night
The bombing, the noise, children screaming in fright.
Terrified families hiding away
Imprisoned in darkness, praying for day.
English territory taken over by German planes in the sky
Aggressive fighters willing to die.
A terrible war ripping the country apart
Destroying families like a punch to the heart.
Nasty and violent, the terrible noise in the air
The end of the war - part of everyone's prayer.
The blackout stops any light from escaping outside
The country united by terror and pride.
Fathers and brothers, uncles and friends join the war
Not all are lucky enough to walk back through the door.
The men in the trenches, how many have died
The women and children all the tears they have cried.
Soldiers everywhere, their uniforms blue or green
Never have so many service men been seen.
Some things can't be forgotten, the suffering and pain
The war will end, but will life ever be the same again?

Katie Dyment (13)
Holywell High School, Holywell

Peaceful Sleep

The world should be peaceful, go to sleep at night
Instead of lots of wars and bombs give us all a great fright
What would it be like if everyone was friends?
But everyone has an enemy, they don't have to pretend.

War causes poverty all over the world
But some people just worry about having their hair straight or curled.
Why don't people think about the bad bits in life?
The heartache and strife.

We could all die if a bomb went off
Then people say that's life, it's just tough.
But if you really think about the death and the hurt
You would always worry and be alert.

When we say we're starving, we have no idea
People in Africa are so hungry, you would shed a tear.
The food that they grow is lost in war
They pray and beg for more.

So please stop all war, arguments and fighting
These people don't need it, they need electric and lighting
Clean sanitation to help keep them healthy
Stop war now, as we are already so wealthy.

Bronwen Edwards (13)
Holywell High School, Holywell

The Creature Under The Sink!

It all started on a normal Monday
At break, on the yard, people start to play
But not for me, I knew something was wrong,
'What's that thing under the sink?' were the lyrics of a child's song
That child was me
I was determined to solve that mystery!

School had started
But the creature had not parted
This was just round one
The creature is as crazy as our neighbour's son
It started to buzz just like a bee
This wasn't going to stop me!

I didn't know what the creature could be
Sometimes it sounded like a possessed monkey
It hissed like a dangerous snake
Should I charge at it with a garden rake?
It made all sorts of bizarre sounds
Rumbles, grumbles, bangs and pounds!

This carried on for a month and a day
Then suddenly it just went away
No more puzzling noises
No more stamping of his toeses
Eventually I solved the mystery
He was a person, just like me!

Danielle Farren (12)
Holywell High School, Holywell

The Howling Horror

As the howling breeze blows through the trees
And the rain trickles on my face
I look around with a steady pace
Ow, what a horrible place.

I walk through a darkened wood
The weary groans
The broken bones
And the puddles of blood.

I get further in
And the horror begins
The blood from my forehead
And my aching shins.

The bats hanging from the staring trees
I get down to my knees
I beg around me, please, please
But there is no answer for me.

Kieran Jones (13)
Holywell High School, Holywell

My Mum

I love my mum she cares for me
She washes my clothes and makes my tea.

She cheers me up when I am sad
And she rarely ever gets mad.

On her face she bears a smile
But does get sad once in a while.

My caring mum is never mean
The best mum I've ever seen.

She lets me bring my friends around
We go to the shop, she gives us a pound.

Every now and then she'll buy me a present
My mum is really very pleasant.

I love my mum she cares for me
She washes my clothes and makes my tea.

Adele Parry (13)
Holywell High School, Holywell

I Have A Dream

I have a dream
Of a world without fear
Where children are smiling
And no crying you hear.

I have a dream
Of a world without war
Where no one is hungry
And there's famine no more.

I have a dream
Of a world without pain
Where those with parched faces
Lift their lips to the rain.

I have a dream
Of a world calm, serene
With nations united
Dreams for each human being.

John Sandham Davies (13)
Holywell High School, Holywell

The Old Flame

You discarded me like a tattered rug
Forgot about me as if I had never existed
Forgot our love as if it had ceased to begin;
You stole my heart
Then threw it back -
Each night I cried until no more tears fell;
I prayed you would come back to me -
Love me as I loved you;
I watched -
As you kissed and danced
With other women
As you tore me up
Looking upon me as a foul old hag;
But now,
Now I have forgotten you -
Thrown you out of my heart;
No longer shall I whine over you,
My soul is free of your love
My head cleared of your memory;
I shall wait no longer
To forgive your broken promises.

Katie Cuthbertson (14)
Kelvinside Academy, Glasgow

My Dear Napoleon

As I sit here with your precious words
And feel the harsh parchment beneath my fingers
I think of all the long days that lie ahead
And yearn for but a single glimpse of you.
My heart aches for your return
For these endless battles to cease
Have you not conquered enough lives?
Do I no longer hold a place in your heart?
For I can no longer fight back my emotions
You are always away
Always distant
Always, always, always.
Your promises have faded
Just like my love for you
And every sorrowful tear that falls
Is like a thousand daggers.
I beg for this pain to end
And yet I cling on
Desperately trying to feel
But I can stand this torture no more.
I need to escape, far, far away
Where my heart can stop for but a second
So that I can forget for just a moment
So that your words can seep from my thoughts
And bleed from my memory.
All I need is to be free for an instant
And I shall leave behind a lifetime.

Yan Ping Lee (14)
Kelvinside Academy, Glasgow

Mrs Einstein

He pulls me closer as we walk
I jerk away and quicken my pace, concentrating on the steps I take
Not wanting to think, not wanting to break.

He, the great scientist, enters the room;
Within seconds I am pushed to the side. Again.
He waves his hand at me, summoning me over to meet his colleagues
So now you want me beside you?

I listen as they talk, looking at the clock, watching it tick.
Finally he nudges me. It's time to go home
For a quiet celebration of our own?
Of course not! It's back to work. Again.

He peers and peers down into the sticky microscope
Is his eye stuck to it?
Only rising to sip his coffee
Placed there by whom?
Before plunging deep back into the silent depths of thought.

He was the one I waited for, I think as I tiptoe back out
The one that I would love till the end of time - so I used to say
Now I say nothing at all.

Part of me wants to stay, to connect to him once more
I want to see his face light up, his eyes sparkle
I stand, frozen by the door, watching him work
Out of boredom. Out of spite.
But I know he'll hardly notice - I can't stand it anymore
Being near him yet blocked out by his world - the one he escapes
                                                    to, now.

He used to escape to another world: our world
How happy it made him to be with me, to get away from all the buzz;
Now he can't wait to get back, I can see it in his face;
Itching to get back to the basement, *he's waiting,* willing
                                        for an excuse to leave
So he can escape me and the shell of our love.

Saskia Livingstone (14)
Kelvinside Academy, Glasgow

Creation

I see light
Filling my heart with confidence and strength
Shining, covering the world in its glorious glow.

I see sky
Careless swirls of colour, a painting of beauty above us
The artists never failing to amaze our souls.

I see the seas
Strong waves burling and crashing into rocks, replaced by white froth
Softly whispering the secrets of the water, beautiful and betraying.

I see land
Mountains reaching into the sky, speaking back
Plants colouring the world with joy and hope.

I see the sun
A burning ball of light, coming and going
Tempting the idle eye to stare in its glory.

I see the moon
Glowing mystically, haunting our dreams until it vanishes
Always changing disguise while watching the world intently.

I see stars
Dreams lighting the night, concealing many secrets
Legends of brave deeds written down for eternity to see.

I see fish
The sea filled with life as streaks of colour dip and dive
While others choose to lurk in the dark depths, waiting.

I see birds
Swooping and soaring, swiftly ruling the open skies
Diving into invisible water, pulling up in the last second.

I see mammals
Large and small, short and tall, covering land
Hiding down holes and in trees, spotted, striped and proud to be
different.

I see man
Smiles and sounds of laughter, hearts filled with happiness
Caring for others, while admiring the world around.

I saw
And it was good.

Charles Houston (13)
Kirkcudbright Academy, Kirkcudbright

Off

I wonder why, that we can fly
Up in the sky on a cherry pie?
Looking At Mars
And all the stars.

Then turning over
At the white cliffs of Dover.
Floating away
On my bed of hay.

I then reach a sign
On it only a line.
Off to a place
With my cardboard box case.

Birds swoop and soar
In verse number four.
It then begins to snow,
Drifting very slow.

Acting a scene,
Eating the cream.
Getting out of my bed
With the sunrise that's red.

Alex Lithgow (13)
Langholm Academy, Langholm

Open Your Eyes

Can you see it? Where? Over there?
Just see it through my eyes   ·
What? The stars race and dance through the night sky
Holding the secrets of time
Blazing in the hearts of young and old
Going as they please
Telling me who I am and where I am in this world
Making it sound so clear
Do you see through that window into my world?

Can you see it? Where? Over there?
Just see it through my eyes
What? The silver wind whistling, so proud and noble
As it swirls and swoops selecting objects
To accompany it on its never-ending journey
Just to show us its might and power
Do you see through that window into my world?

Can you see it? Where? Over there?
Just see it through my eyes
What? The ground cool to the touch and loved so much
As the forest so dark and deep
Looming in the shadows of the mountain
Directing the air, cool and crisp
So pure is this place I live in
Do you see through that window into my world?

Can you see it? Where? Over there?
Just see it through my eyes
What? The spirits whisking me away
Longing for my friendship, so mysterious and full of flair
It's hard to resist their impression upon my delicate state of mind
How they fascinate me with the threads of life
Now do you see through that window into my world?
Can you see it? Where? Over there?
Just see it through my eyes

What? You can't see what I see
For it is my imagination, so simple and pure
Where I can escape this complex world known as reality
My imagination holds the key to my soul
For I am the only one who can see through the eyes
And the window into my world.

Stephanie Cartner (13)
Langholm Academy, Langholm

Granny Pat

Granny Pat has bad dreams,
Granny Pat often screams.
She rolls about all night long,
Singing her favourite Abba songs.

The 'Dancing Queen' never stops,
For a microphone she uses mops.
Up and down the stairs all night,
Until the windows let in light.

Then she hobbles back to bed
And crawls back in with Grandpa Ted.
Then gets up at 8 o'clock
And on the door she hears a knock.

It's old Bill from next door,
Last night he heard Ted snore.
He said if this snoring never stops
He'll turn him in to the cops.

But Granny Pat has a trick or two,
She made Grandpa Ted sleep in the loo.
She wouldn't let him out at all,
While Granny Pat had a ball.

Singing, dancing all night long,
Dancing to that Abba song,
But in the morning at the bar
She does know
Last night she was a star!

Jamie Fletcher (13)
Langholm Academy, Langholm

Cheltenham Gold Cup

I've just come out of the paddock
And cantered to the start,
I'm nervous, my heart's thumping,
The starting judge is ready for us,
We're up the line and . . .

We're off,
I've taken the lead,
Oh yes, I love the fences,
I'm up to the jump,
A horse has clipped me from behind,
There's a few riders off.

I'm up to the 10th
And really tired,
But I'll still jump the same,
Ow, I've cut my legs on the brush
We have to stay close.

We're now coming to the famous Cheltenham hill
And jumping the last, weeeeee
I'm over safely and have taken the lead
I've been smacked into a firm gallop
Past the blur of screaming and to the post
And . . .
I've won!

I'm getting loads of cheers,
The stable lad's got me now,
Back into the paddock,
Here's my trainer, Frankie,
With my rug, yes!

Here's the announcement,
Winner of the Cheltenham Gold Cup,
Amberleigh House.

Kieran McLean Johnstone (13)
Langholm Academy, Langholm

The Random World Of Dreams!

At night when you are sleeping
Your fantasy world evolves
Events exaggerated
Ready to unfold.

A dream when you are running
But never get too far.
A dream where you see things
Like you're on another planet.

A dream that is not a dream;
Scary secrets shine through.
A dream where you are walking
And end up in another room.

A dream where something happens
A warning for the future
Are these dreams really true?
You'll have to wait until morning!

Lisa Rajszys (13)
Langholm Academy, Langholm

Time Machine

As I look to the stars and close my eyes,
I wonder how the future will go by?

Will people still go to school?
Will there still be so many rules?

Will hands still be used to write?
Will eyes still be used for sight?

Flowers might turn silver and gold
People might not turn old.

I wonder if the Earth will still go around,
I wonder if fish will make a sound?

So many things can change -
The world is going to be so strange!

Hayley Bell (13)
Langholm Academy, Langholm

A Black And White Photograph Of A Rainbow

Peering through a looking glass,
I saw myself
Looking at a rainbow.

A rainbow of beauty and emotions,
Of the future and fortune,
Love and passion.

A crack and everything was lost,
Now there was only me
And a rainbow.

A dull and suffering rainbow,
A dark rainbow of shadows,
Dread and regrets.

Now splinters of mirror fill my dream,
Each trapping a multicoloured memory.

Katie Smart (13)
Langholm Academy, Langholm

Falling Into Darkness

Lying in my dream dreaming,
Dreaming that I'm falling into the sea
It is shouting my name,
Ready to swallow me whole into its dark world
I can see people staring down at me
Lifeless as a heron hunting its meal
I'm yelling out at them
But they just stare,
Waiting for me to fall to my death
I try to reach out to grab onto something, anything
But I'm too far out, so I turn
And look down to the waiting sea
I'm nearly there, so I could 5, 4, 3, 2, 1 . . .
I'm not there anymore
Waiting to be swallowed by the sea
I'm in my bed lying sweating.

Ben Norris (14)
Langholm Academy, Langholm

The Peace Of The Countryside

Lying on the hills
With wind in my hair
Sun beaming soft and warm
The valleys quiet, no sound at all.

The sheep are clouds
In the green grassy sky
Heather like brown splashes of brown
My eyes are closing from the sun.

It is like a hot bun out of an oven
The smell of nature's perfume
I breathe it in well, cooling my lungs
Birds are singing in rhythm to a number one song
As I take my last breath, I wake up to the realistic world.

Russell Anderson (13)
Langholm Academy, Langholm

I'm First There

There, in the blazing sun
Sitting, nothing to do
Nothing to say.

Children go to school
Only the lucky ones though
Someone sleeping on the pavement.

Some in scruffy clothes
As thin as a pencil line
Porridge for breakfast, lunch and dinner
How boring that must be.

Footballers thinking of themselves
Some, £70,000 a week, what about me?
If only I could change my life.

Iain Little (13)
Langholm Academy, Langholm

Locked In Perfection

What has become of the modern world?
Make-up, celebrity and skinniness,
This has become the modern beauty -
Dyed hair, skeletal figures and lipgloss
Brainwashed into our young generation,
Drag queen make-up
The sex craze
No flesh just bones
And bleached hair
This is the new perfection.

Free the world
Free the young generation of all this nonsense
I dream of a non-perfect world
That would be perfect.

Let's all have luscious, fake blonde hair
Piercings, long nails and orange blusher.
Let's all wear clothes that are hardly clothes at all.
Forget the reading,
Let's live in the magazine,
This is what's happening to our new generation,
Helpless and vulnerable.

Free the world
Free the new generation of all this nonsense
I dream of a non-perfect world
That would be perfect.

Jade Graham (13)
Langholm Academy, Langholm

It's My Dream, Go Away!

It's my dream, go away!
I want it to myself
Everyone just bullies me
Like a little elf.

The walls are made of cushions
And angels fly all day
If only you weren't here
Just please go away!

Here, police don't exist
Except the butcher's lad
Who never has a job to do
Unless you are bad.

It's my dream, go away!
Everyone is polite
Why not go down to the park
And maybe fly your kite?

It's my dream, go away!
This is my dreamland
The one I dreamt on my own
Leave now at my command!

Actually, now I think I'm lonely
Oh look, there's Uncle Kevin
I really don't want you to leave here now
To me, this is Heaven.

Glen Cavers (13)
Langholm Academy, Langholm

Snowflakes

Snowflakes make the place
Turn into a blanket of snow
It is as cold as ice
But I like to go sledging on it.

Snowflakes, snowflakes
How I like them
They are good for snowmen
And for snowballs
Each piece of winter snow
That is a 6-pointed star
Is a shade of white
And it is so fun to play with
Snowflakes remind me of Christmas
And all the presents you get.

I like to hear the snow
Crunch under my feet
I like to see the snow
Fall from the cloudy sky
And then when it turns to sleet
I go inside
And all the fun is over.

Luke Paterson (12)
Langholm Academy, Langholm

Snowflakes

Snow has a touch
Like no other
Its delicate touch
Only in winter

As white as paper
As cold as ice
As smooth as a crystal
As sharp as a spike

Snowball fights with my friends
Wonderful times
Brilliant memories

As funny as a clown
As fun as friends
As slow as a turtle

Is a good time of year
When the snow appears
As clear as glass
As shiny as silver

One piece of snow left
As small as me.

Daniel Johnstone (12)
Langholm Academy, Langholm

The Old House On The Hill

The old house stands still on the hill
Where nobody ever goes
As the wind blows the house shakes
As if there was an earthquake
It's all lonely in the house on the hill.

As you walk up it gets colder and colder
It hits your face as fast as Concorde
As the cold hits your eyes you start to cry
As you get halfway you feel
Like a block of ice from the Arctic.

Now you're nearly at the top
You start to melt, you are getting warmer
Every step you take
When you reach the big gates
The question comes to mind
Which path should I take?

Finally, you reach the house
You open the door *and* walk across the creaky floorboards
Lolling out *of* the window at the little village
That is why it is called the house on the hill
Because it is so high.

Leisha Thirtle (13)
Langholm Academy, Langholm

Snowflakes

Snowflakes falling from the sky
As slow as a snail
As dark as a six-pointed star
Snowflakes falling from the high winter sky
White snowflakes falling from the sky
I feel like throwing *snowballs!*

Maria Bell (12)
Langholm Academy, Langholm

Lonely House Of Darkness

Worn and crooked
Years of isolation made it this way
Night has covered it like a blanket but it is still too cold.

The windows are eyes
Hard to see through
Years of neglect have made it this way
The stars above are together but the house is alone.

A broken chair sits alone in the shadows by itself
Years of laughter and company all gone
The moon is like a torch shining
On the soft, rotten wood of the door.

The paint peels like an orange
Years of dampness made it this way
The house is crying
It will stay like this forever beneath the dark sky.

Katrina Fung (13)
Langholm Academy, Langholm

Snowflakes

The six-pointed star
Falls so silent
In the dead of night
Falls on my car
As gentle as a butterfly
The six-pointed star
Glides so far
Then lands at my window
The six-pointed star
Looks so bizarre
But yet graceful
The six-pointed star.

Kieran Green (12)
Langholm Academy, Langholm

My World

My world is a place I can be happy
My world is a place I can be sad
A place I can be me
A place I can be free

My world is a place I can scream
My world is a place I can whisper
A place I can be me
A place I can be free

My world can be filled with colour
My world can be black and white
A place I can be free
A place I can be me

My world can be exciting
My world can be dull
A place I can be me
A place that I want to be.

Alistair Little (13)
Langholm Academy, Langholm

Snowflakes

Snowflakes, snowflakes
Cold and sparkling snowflakes
Snowflakes, snowflakes
Fall so far from the sky
Snowflakes, snowflakes
Have six points
Snowflakes, snowflakes
Are white and glittery
Snowflakes, snowflakes
Are as small as a mouse.

Aimée Maxwell (12)
Langholm Academy, Langholm

The Broken Dream

The dreams are no longer scary
The dream catcher stores them all;
How sad it must feel if it were living.

The dreams I drift into
I love him so much
He's always there with me
Always close enough to touch.

He keeps me out of the rain
It could be real
We speak so much
Yet we talk without words

The next night I just can't wait for.
He'll be there once my eyes close tight.
Same place.
Similar time.

But no, where is he?
He's no longer there.
Has he forgotten me?
My heart starts to tear.

If he were here
He would fix my heart.
He would use anything
Sellotape would do.

I see him, I can't wait
But he runs and runs
The wind no longer blows in his hair.
I get soaked by the rain.

I wake up
No way
The thread's torn
The dream catcher gone.
Here come the nightmares.

Hannah Cumming (13)
Langholm Academy, Langholm

School's Nearly Over

School's nearly over, don't know what to do
Going through doors, searching for a clue
Talking to teachers in my thinking mode
Too many answers, I'm about to explode.

When I leave I want to be rich
With billions and billions of pounds
And join a rock band
With all the best sounds.

I'll travel the world, day by day
I'll stop in America to visit Peter Kay
We'll start up a business to entertain the world
Too late, it was only a dream.

Can dreams come true? I don't know
A million pounds and a mansion for you
This is a secret between you and me
They can come true if you want them to.

I wake up early in the morning
Looking forward to living in luxury.

Adam Park (14)
Langholm Academy, Langholm

A Dream Of Hell

I had that dream again
Where Hell is on Earth
Tormented souls being torn apart
And every wish, just out of reach.

Demons around every corner
Just waiting for you to pass by
People calling for my help
But all I can do is watch.

And the one who is ordering this pain
Is just like the Devil
With a spear in one hand
And a person in the other

This dream I have is never-ending
Every night it happens again
Until the morning's light wakes me
Half-tortured to tears.

Aaron Tedham (13)
Langholm Academy, Langholm

I'm Dreaming Of Dreaming

My mum told me I've no imagination
I can't dream, Daddy says
I'd love to dream
I'd build a paradise of palaces
Fairy princesses and kings
Unicorns and elves would rule the land
I'd be a lady with golden hair
I'd be a queen's daughter
I'd play the harp beautifully
I'd like to be rescued from towers tall
By courtiers strong and handsome
The fairest of the land would be me
Trolls and giants non-existent
Gingerbread men at every corner
Showing the way round this fairyland
There'd be no shortage of money
Nobody'd give a damn about weight
The world would revolve around happiness
No tax collectors or mortgages to pay
Nobody would be enemies
We'd all be friends
Pixies wouldn't be a rare sight.

I'd love to be able to dream about this
But I can't dream, Daddy says so
And Mum says I've no imagination.

Beth Brooks-Taylor (13)
Langholm Academy, Langholm

Dreaming Of A Nightmare

Wake up Monday
Dare I look in the mirror?
Hair over my eyes
Hopefully they won't see me.

Down the school halls, Tuesday lunch
Head low like a dying flower.
Tumble to the ground,
Maybe it was just an accident.

Only Wednesday
Can I take much more?
Can't tell what I'm feeling
Completely alone.

When Thursday comes
I'm ready to give in
So tired of this life
I need my solitude.

Friday has arrived
The last day of torment.
I'll be away from these people
In a world of my own.

This nightmare I long for
It's stuck in my head.
Memories replaying,
Why can't I go back?

Trapped in this world of perfection,
Forbidden to say my true feelings
Fake smiles and make-up
Why can't I just wake up?

Zoe Ellis (13)
Langholm Academy, Langholm

Snowy Dream

I look down the mountain
See the icicles
Like a frozen fountain

I feel petrified
I thought about it
And took a deep sigh

I was ready!

I pushed the ski poles
In the snow
And dodged the random murky hole

The odd jump
I feel I want to stop and then
I land with a bump

I'm happy to be here
The air is blowing in my face
And under my hat I cannot hear

At the bottom I see my friend
I make a cheesy grin
And finally I'm at the end

I finish and I'm so happy
I've done it
I'm ready to do it again, snappy!

Sophie Cutteridge (13)
Langholm Academy, Langholm

The Singing Doughnut Attack

It was a busy market
I was plodding down the street
Eyes were going side to side
Looking for the friend I had to meet.

There was a baker selling doughnuts
I was hungry so I bought one
I heard another down the street
Shouting, 'Get your rock buns!'

I saw the friend I needed
Then someone started to sing
I looked down and saw the doughnut
Which was singing 'My Favourite Things'!

The baker's was a jukebox
Each doughnut had a different song
But when I listened carefully
The key was totally wrong.

The doughnuts hopped down from the stand
And started charging down the street
The musical menaces were heading straight
Into a stall selling sweets.

There was a gun on the floor
A doughnut held it to my head
It slowly pulled the trigger
And I found myself in bed.

Hayden Goodfellow (13)
Langholm Academy, Langholm

Angels Calling

He was in a battlefield;
Bullets pinging,
Bombs exploding.
On a French beach,
His allies were being blown to bits.
Next to him people were being gunned down rapidly
Numbers from 100 to 1 in the blink of an eye.
He was alone,
Whizz, whizz, whizz
A bullet shot by his head -
A bullet shot by his arm -
Squirt - blood was coming out of his chest.
He'd been shot.

The angels were calling to him
He was rising into the air
He woke up lying in bed
Tomato soup on his chest from the night before.

Dean Cartner (13)
Langholm Academy, Langholm

Fight

The silence of the black
Is pressing all around you
A shot, a shout, a rustle
You need to see the night-time through
Keep fear at bay, and come what may
Don't cry about the dark.

The enemy's sharpening its claws
The seconds seem too long
Your heartbeat's pounding in your throat
You will suffer if you are wrong
The fight is hard, but be on your guard
You can't cry about the dark.

There's bullets above and bodies below
I know it's scary on your own
That could be you rotting underfoot
But only a coward wants to moan
Breathe if you dare, but you must take care
Not to cry about the dark.

Where there was a future, there's only now
Where's there was life, there's just cold hard steel
Do the dead need your tears?
It doesn't matter how you feel
It's kill or die, and this is why
They cried about the dark.

Rosie Dahlstrom (14)
Largs Academy, Largs

February Night

Steamy mist hovers
heavily around houses,
the telephone wires
stretched out across the sky
stand out black.
Six.

The car drives past;
yellow,
then
red.

Floating smudges of
street lamps waver
and sharp air
coats the

night. Tiny bubbles of rain
paint the

window sill. And the
cackling
geese; where are
they?

The house opposite is in darkness.

Rosie Beardon (16)
Lockerbie Academy, Lockerbie

Unicorn

U nderneath the deep, dark mountains

N obody knew, nobody had seen

I rridescent eyes as they sparkle

C ounting down the men that tried

O verlooking their tragic mystery

R earing as the creature took our fear

N obody knew, nobody had seen.

Anna Thomson (13)
Lossiemouth High School, Lossiemouth

Pengar

P enguin, crab and demon spawn

E very child that is born

N ever lived until this day

G reatness beats him down

A demonic screech taking fear from the night

R eaping breath, bringing death, no more light, his last fight.

Tony Walber (13)
Lossiemouth High School, Lossiemouth

Young Writers Information

We hope you have enjoyed reading this book - and that you will continue to enjoy it in the coming years.

If you like reading and writing poetry drop us a line, or give us a call, and we'll send you a free information pack.

Alternatively if you would like to order further copies of this book or any of our other titles, then please give us a call or log onto our website at www.youngwriters.co.uk

**Young Writers Information
Remus House
Coltsfoot Drive
Peterborough
PE2 9JX**

(01733) 890066